Don't
Be
No
Fool . . .

Don't
Be
No
Fool . . .

Read and Study the Word of God for Yourself

Brother William A. Swinton

authorHOUSE®

AuthorHouse™
1663 Liberty Drive
Bloomington, IN 47403
www.authorhouse.com
Phone: 1-800-839-8640

Published by AuthorHouse   11/06/2012

ISBN: 978-1-4772-8674-6 (sc)
ISBN: 978-1-4772-8673-9 (e)

Library of Congress Control Number: 2012920676

Dedication

I, William A. Swinton, Dedicate this book to Almighty GOD, through my Lord and Savior, Jesus Christ. Amen.

Special Thanks

To: Mrs. Neitha McDonald for obeying;

Proverbs 22:6.

From: William A. Swinton, your loving grandson.

Contents

Foreword

This book has been written for people of all walks of life. The information found in the following pages is for you, The Babe in Christ, you, The Grown-up Christian and also for you, The Non-Believer.

This book points out and addresses a lot of issues concerning Faith, Trust and Belief, in the Almighty GOD.

The words of this book, if taken to heart, can instruct, guide and edify you in your initial walk and subsequent journey through this life as a Christian.

Please read this book along with your Bible as the main purpose of this book is to encourage you, the Reader, to Read and Study, the Word of GOD, for yourself.

All of the scriptures used in the writing of this book are taken from the Holy Bible **(King James Version)** and are written with the understanding given to the author through the anointing of the Holy Spirit.

For the person who reads this book and heeds its message, I'm sure that GOD Almighty will bless you accordingly. For those who are Non-Believers or not sure what to believe, I have a suggestion. Before trying anything else, try GOD! Don't Be No Fool, please read and study the Word of GOD, for yourself.

Prayer

Heavenly and merciful Father, first of all, please allow me to thank you and praise you for inspiring me to write this book.

I humbly ask that you allow this book to be a blessing to all that read and receive these words and apply them in their lives.

I also ask that you bless this book in such a way that it will bring forth good fruit to the Glory of your Kingdom; thirty, sixty, even one hundred fold.

It is in the name of my Lord and Savior, Jesus Christ, that I ask you, praise you and thank you. Amen.

Preface

This book has been written by someone who should not be considered as a professional writer. Again, the main purpose of this book is to encourage the reader to read and study the Word of God for themselves.

Each chapter of this book contains this same message, however, each chapter has been written to bring an awareness of a number of important issues that are commonly misunderstood, through lack of knowledge of the Word of GOD.

It is my earnest and honest prayer that you read and receive the messages of this book, so that you don't fall victim to the same misconceptions that have cost so many people their lives and ultimately their souls.

No part of this book has been written based on the opinion or imagination of the author. All of the personal experiences written about in this book are true. The Title of this book, the Titles of all ten chapters as well as all of the scriptures used in the writing of this book were given to the author by GOD, through the Holy Spirit.

This book has been manifest into reality for your education as well as edification. Just as I have received a blessing through writing this book, you, too, will receive a blessing if you read and also receive its message. No doubt, I will be praying, in the name of Jesus Christ, to that end.

In the **15ᵗʰ Chapter of the book of Matthew, verses 8 and 9**, gives us a basis for a book such as this. At any point, before or after reading this book, I ask that you take five minutes from your busy schedule and read these particular scriptures.

Your reaction to these scriptures can only result in one of two ways, Eternal Life or Eternal Death.

Just in case you don't have your Bible handy, here is **Matthew 15:8 and 9;**

8) This people draweth nigh unto me with their mouth, and honoreth me with their lips; but their heart is far from me.

9) But in vain they do worship me, teaching for doctrines the commandments of men.

May GOD grant a blessing to the readers, hearers and doers of His Holy Word, in Jesus name, I pray. Amen.

Chapter #1

Often imitated, but never Duplicated

In the first chapter of this book, with the help of the Holy Spirit, I will attempt to point out to you some of the things I call imitations of the real thing. The real thing is a religion that is based on the Words of the one and only true and wise GOD. Imitations of the real thing are those that are described by GOD as being false.

Some readers of this book may not agree with what I'm saying but that does not and will not change the Word of GOD. I am confident that the Words of GOD are all true.

Based on my natural and spiritual experiences in life and religion, I have seen a lot of what I call imitations of the real thing. There are many religions of this world that are just that, of this world. They are not real and certainly not true.

In fact, there are even Christian religions that are based on the doctrines of man and not on the Word of GOD. Of course, this renders these religions null and void. Also these religions are categorized as false religions. They are only imitations.

Where did all of these imitations come from? Satan of course, the Father of Lies. His plan is cleverly hidden in these worldly and ungodly religions. His plan has always been the same, to steal, kill and destroy.

Let's examine this a little closer so that there will be no misunderstandings. Satan has the ability to imitate the things that GOD has created in order to, first, steal your mind, second, and kill Your body and last but certainly not least, destroy your soul. This is why so many people fall victim to the so called religions of the world without ever realizing what they really are, of the world.

People's honest and earnest beliefs are being used by Satan to lure and even trap them into a false religion. People also suffer; even die, for lack of knowledge of the Word of GOD.

They rely on what they are told and never or rarely read and study the Word of GOD for themselves.

You've heard the stories about Jonestown, depending on your age, or about the religious group known as the Branch Davidians. These people, for lack of knowledge of the Word of GOD, fell victim to the ranting and ravings of what was clearly, spiritual wickedness, in high places. They were then seduced into believing the imitations of the real thing.

What exactly is an imitation? My understanding is that it is a copy of the real thing but doesn't have the quality of the real thing. In other words, it's a fake, it's not real! We see this concept in a lot of natural things as well as spiritual. Remember, a cubic zirconium is not a true diamond, but it most certainly appears as one to someone who doesn't know or study jewelry.

Did you notice the words know or study? This is the key to spotting fakes or imitations. This principle not only works in spotting fakes or imitations in the natural world but in the spiritual world of religions as well.

In order to choose a real and true Christian religion you must know how to spot the fakes or imitations. The only way that this can be accomplished is by reading and studying the Word of GOD for yourself.

No one can tell you more about GOD than GOD Himself. GOD reveals Himself in His Word. By His Word, GOD makes His thoughts, understandings and truths known to us. He also tells us how to worship Him; "In spirit and in truth".

GOD Himself knows how Satan operates. He knows that there are fake and imitation religions in and of this world. In fact, He has warned us in His Word. If we were to read and study His Word we would know what He has to say about fake and imitation religions.

As I read and studied the Word of GOD, I noticed a scripture that simply said this; **Romans 3:4 says,**

> **3) GOD forbid: yea, let God be true, but every man a liar, as it is written, THAT THOU MIGHTEST BE JUSTIFIED IN THY SAYINGS, AND MIGHTEST OVERCOME WHEN THOU ART JUDGED.**

Why do you think GOD said this? He knows that if you don't read and study His Word for your self and just take what men say about worshiping Him, you could easily be fooled by fake or imitation men of God who claim to be serving GOD, but are really seeking to be served. Here are two examples of what I'm saying, Jim Jones and David Koresh.

Now I'm not putting these men down, no, not at all. My heart went out to them because they were deceived and destroyed along with most of their followers. In both of these cases, people put all of their trust and belief in what a man said and by doing so, neglected what GOD said. Would you believe me instead of GOD? Although I'm writing this book I don't want you to take my word for what I'm telling you. Instead, I want you to read and study the Word of GOD, for yourself.

If the followers of these two men, not only of these two men as there are many who follow men. If they had only read and studied the Word of GOD for themselves, they would not have been led away, trapped or even destroyed.

To a person who reads and studies the Word of GOD, the entire notion of moving away to some far away location or isolated area, would have been clearly seen as not the will or way of GOD. Remember, the truths about serving GOD can be found in His Word. As people who profess and confess to serve and worship GOD we are not to be hidden.

In **Matthew 5:16**, the Word of GOD says;

16) Let your light so shine before men, that they may see your good works, and glorify your Father which is in heaven.

All those that sold their possessions and either moved to Waco, Texas; or the island of Guyana, bought into an imitation of the real thing. As you can see, the lack of knowledge of the Word of GOD can not only be dangerous, but deadly as well, in this world and beyond. Indeed you need to read and study the Word of God for yourself.

As we continue to look at imitations, we see all kinds of similarities, but here again that's all they are, similarities, they are still imitations. Worldly religions or false religions have similar elements of the real thing. They worship, pray, fast and fellowship, they're imitating.

As I mentioned before its Satan who is behind these worldly or false religions, as you can see they imitate the practices of a Godly religion, the real thing.

I remember once while I was in prayer, in a public but private area. A young man of another religious belief entered the room. The first time this happened I was just finishing up my personal praise, worship and prayer time with GOD. I told the young man to come on in because I was finished. He said; "O.K, but first I have to go cleanse myself". I said, "O.K". As I left the room I thought to my self, with a smile, "My GOD says come as you are".

The next time this happened, the young man came in and again, as before, I was just finishing up my personal praise, worship and prayer time with GOD. I told him to come on in, I was yielding to him. He said; "Well were worshiping the same God anyway, just by a different name". I thought to myself; "Now he done gone and lost his mind"! He didn't know the truth! I quickly said to him; "No, there is a major difference".

After a moment of small talk we decided to meet early the next night so that we could discuss our different views in more detail. Listen very carefully to what I'm about to tell you, it could save not only your life but your soul as well.

The next night came and I was ready for him. I was ready to tell this young fellow the Good News about my Lord and Savior, Jesus Christ, to convert him, to change his belief that we served the same GOD. I was ready, but I kept my cool. When he entered the room, I didn't pounce on him and beat him over the head with my Bible, I sat back and allowed him to come to me.

We started to talk and he admitted or confessed that he was a Muslim. I said, "Yea, that's what I thought". Just as I was about to try to explain to this young man that we did not serve the same GOD, in walks another young man, whom I'm sure

Satan had sent in to disrupt the conversation. Now this young man, the second one, seeing my Bible in my hand, asked if he could see it for a moment. I thought to myself, well maybe he had to come to help. To my surprise, he closed the Bible and focused on the cover. He then pointed at the words; **Holy Bible**, pointing to each letter, he recited the following, "**H**e **O**nly **L**eft **Y**ou, **B**asic **I**nstructions **B**efore **L**eaving **E**arth".

Well, that was it. I told him; "Now that was a nice little anecdote but the real message is on the inside".

Anyhow, the first young man, the confessed Muslim, smiled and said he had to go. I was a bit angered to say the least.

I viewed this young man as in fishing terms, as the one that got away. I told you this to show you how Satan will only allow some people to see the outside of the Bible and no more. This young man, the confessed Muslim, has fallen under the assumption and belief that the Almighty GOD and Allah are one in the same.

You see he has been tricked into believing the lies of Satan who doesn't want to see the inside of the Bible, where he can read and study the Word of GOD and find out that, serving, praising, worshiping or even praying to Allah, will send him straight to Hell.

In the Word of GOD is the truth, the whole truth and nothing but the truth. In the book of **1**st **John 5:19, 20 and 21**, scripture says;

19) And we know that we are of God, and the whole world lieth in wickedness.

20) And we know that the Son of God is come, and hath given us an understanding that we may know him that is true, and we are in him that is true, even in his Son Jesus Christ. This is the true God, and eternal life.

21) Little children keep yourselves from idols. Amen.

Now do you understand how important it is for you to read and study the Word of GOD for yourself? In the scriptures you just read, GOD has spoken very clearly to all people. He has removed any and all doubt as to whom the true GOD is and at the same time warned us to keep away from idols, false gods.

People seem to think that a name is not really that important. No doubt this is a lie told to them by Satan as it is contrary to the Word of GOD. **Acts 4:12** says;

12) Neither is there salvation in any other: for there is none other name given among men, whereby we must be saved.

The name that is being referred to is none other than, Jesus Christ. Now isn't that wonderful? Sure if you know this, even better if you believe it. But what if you don't?

In the book of **Matthew, 4:19**, Jesus is speaking to Simon (called Peter) and his brother Andrew,

19) And he saith unto them, Follow me, and I will make you fisher of men.

I believe Jesus said this because he knew that people needed to be caught, or hooked.

Before ending this chapter, I would like to call to your attention another cleverly disguised imitation of the real thing. When I looked at one of the most pronounced so called Godly religions in the world today, I was amazed at the degree of deviation from what I had read and studied in the Word of GOD.

Now this is different from the young man who was a confessed Muslim. These people are confessed believers in the Almighty GOD. As I watched and listened to their religious practices, I saw and heard a lot of the doctrines of man and little of GOD.

What I'm about to tell you may rub some people the wrong way. If this is the case, that's fine. I'm sure you heard the expression, the truth hurts. It is not my intentions to hurt anyone, only to tell you the truth; a truth that is based only on the Word of GOD and not my own opinion.

Now listen to this and see if you can tell which religious groups I'm referring to. They make it a practice of calling their religious leaders father. It's evident that these people and more importantly their leaders place more emphasis on their own man made doctrines and beliefs, than they do the Word of GOD.

First of all, this is what the Word of GOD has to say about calling a religious leader father; **Matthew 23:9** says:

9) And call no man your father upon the earth: for one is your Father, which is in heaven.

Did you get that? Then let me backup to **Matthew 23:8**, it says;

8) But be not ye called Rabbi: for one is your Master, even Christ, and all ye are brethren.

I can understand how some people can be misled, they're leaders are misleading them. Again, these kinds of errors wouldn't be made if people would just read and study the Word of GOD, for themselves.

I'm not done yet, there is still more I need to tell you. Have you ever heard the expression; "Blind leading the blind"? Friends this is exactly what's happening in the world today. People join churches and worship GOD so that ultimately their souls will be saved. This saving or salvation we seek is from the wrath of God's anger. We must take heed to His Word or we will, for lack of knowledge of His Word, suffer with the Non-believers.

Is this really what you want? If you answer no to this question, then please read and study the Word of GOD for yourself.

In the Word of GOD you'll find that Jesus Christ Himself, didn't, "Hail Mary", His own mother. The truth is written in the Word of GOD about how He reacted when he was told that His mother was outside and wanted to see Him. Scripture says in **Matthew 12: 46 thru 50**;

46) While he yet talked to the people, behold, his mother and his brethren stood without, desiring to speak with him.

47) Then one said unto him, Behold, thy mother and thy brethren stand without, desiring to speak with thee.

48) But he answered and said unto him that told him, Who is my mother? and who are my brethren?

49) And he stretched forth his hand toward his disciples, and said, Behold my mother and brethren!

50) For whososever shall do the will of my Father which is in heaven, the same is my brother, and sister, and mother.

Once again, do you see the difference between the doctrines and practices of man and the Word of GOD? How can people not see and hear these imitations? Simply put, they don't read and study the Word of GOD for themselves.

As I write the words of this book, by the inspiration of the Holy Spirit, it is my sincere prayer that you receive from the Almighty

GOD, through my Lord and Savior, Jesus Christ, the wisdom, knowledge and understanding you need to be able to spot these and any other imitations of the real thing.

The real thing that I have referred to in this chapter is none other than a religion that acknowledges the Almighty GOD as the creator of Heaven and Earth and the fullness thereof. That He gave His only begotten Son, Jesus Christ, out of His sincere love for us. That whoever would believe in Him, would not perish, but have everlasting life.

I hope and pray that this chapter will bring forth, Glory, Honor and Praise to GOD, from the reader and a desire to read and study the Word of GOD so that He will be worshipped in Spirit and Truth.

Please take these words to heart as they are true. Also take note that Satan is out to deceive all people, to coin a phrase; "By any means necessary". I want you to keep these truths in mind as you seek the Kingdom of GOD and all its righteousness, and know that GOD's real and true religion is: **Often Imitated, But Never Duplicated.**

Chapter #2

Seeing Is Believing?

Abracadabra, Alakazam! Do you remember these words? They are usually associated with magicians and their tricks. These words seem to add to the suspense of the magical trick being performed. Hopefully we are at the age that we know that it's a trick, slight of hand, mirrors, trap doors, etc. Nevertheless, our eyes, ears and other senses all agree, its magic, when in reality we have been tricked, fooled.

In this next chapter, as always, with the help of the Holy Spirit, I will attempt to lead you into the truth with no tricks. As far as the magic tricks are concerned, we sit and watch in amazement and although it's not real, we believe in what we see. I want you to keep this in mind as we continue through this chapter.

In the first chapter of this book I tried my best to drive home the point of reading and studying the Word of GOD for yourself. If you noticed, I provided for you scriptures by location. I did this so that you could easily find these scriptures as you read and study the Word of GOD for yourself.

As I started to seek the kingdom of GOD and all its righteousness, I discovered a lot of promises in the Word of GOD. I'm like most of us, I like to be promised something, especially if it's from someone I believe is honest and will keep their word. This alone brings about a belief in the promise which creates expectancy.

Those of you who have children had better be 100% sure that you can make good on a promise made to them or you will be sorry you ever opened your mouth, agreed? Now with the same components of promise and expectancy we find in the natural, we also find in the spiritual.

What links these two components together in the natural is belief. Children believe in our promises and become expectant.

This same principle should be used in the spiritual world as well. As you read and study the Word of GOD, you will also find certain scriptures in which GOD is making a promise to us. Remember, I told you before that the Words of GOD are all true, whether we choose to believe them or not. I choose to believe and I can testify that GOD keeps His Word as well as His promises.

One thing is for sure, you'll never know until you try Him. For example, **Matthew 7:7** says;

> **7) Ask, and it shall be given you; seek, and ye shall find; knock, and it shall be opened unto you**.

Sure sounds good to me. Now keep in mind that this is a promise from the Almighty GOD, He can't lie. He keeps His promises and we can surely trust Him. But wait, there is more!

In **Matthew 7:8**, GOD explains to whom this promise is given;

> **8) For everyone that asketh receiveth; and he that seeketh findeth; and to him that knocketh it shall be opened.**

GOD makes Himself very clear and is careful to confirm this promise. He gives us a comparison using our relationship with our own children to express His attitude about giving to us.

GOD says in **Matthew 7:9 thru 11**;

9) Or what man is there of you, whom if his son ask bread, will he give him a stone?

10) Or if he ask a fish, will he give him a serpent?

11) If ye then, being evil, know how to give good gifts to your children, how much more shall your Father which is in heaven give good things to them that ask him?

Well, there you have it. GOD has given us a promise and a confirmation. All that's needed is for us to provide the belief. In fact, I want you to look at it like this. As I mentioned earlier, when you promise your children something, they believe you and expect you to deliver. We are to view or receive the promises of GOD in this same way.

Before I go any further, do you see what you miss when you don't read and study the Word of GOD for yourself?

We have read the promise. So what must we do in order to receive? First, we must ask! Not just any old way. We must ask the way GOD has instructed us to. This is just as important as asking. GOD took the time to give us specific instructions. I believe He did this to identify who is asking. People who ask according to His will and His way can expect results.

There are basically two types of believers. One who hears the Word of GOD and abides in it, and those who hear the Word of God and ignore it. To those who hear the Word of God and abide in it, GOD has given this assurance.

In **John 14:12 thru 14**, the Word of GOD says;

12) Verily, verily, I say unto you, He that believeth on me, the works that I do shall he do also; and greater works than these shall he do; because I go unto my Father.

13) And whatsoever ye shall ask in my name, that will I do, that the Father may be glorified in the Son.

14) If ye shall ask anything in my name, I will do it.

What is the correct name? It's none other than, Jesus Christ. When you read and study the Word of GOD you will find that these were the instructions that Jesus Christ gave to his disciples. These instructions are for us also if we follow Him. We are to ask for, whatsoever, we want or need of GOD, in the name of Jesus Christ.

Also, the **15ᵗʰ Chapter of John, verse 7** says;

7) If ye abide in me and words abide in you, ye shall ask what ye will, and it shall be done unto you.

Hold it a moment! Before you fall to your knees and start asking GOD for any and everything you can think of, you should always remember whom you are asking for whatsoever. What I want you to understand is that GOD is HOLY! He will only give you those things that have His approval.

Here is a natural example. Everything your child ask you for may not be in you child's best interest. When your child asks you for something you reserve the right to deny any request that you believe may not be to your child's benefit. More or less, there are three possible answers you can give to your child; Yes, No or Wait. Did you get all of that?

Just in case you didn't quite get the full understanding, here is a truth you should consider before asking GOD for whatsoever. We must not ask GOD for things that are un-Godly.

Examine for yourself what it is you are asking. Sisters, GOD will not give you someone else's husband and Brothers; He won't give you someone else's wife. Just be mindful that GOD is HOLY. Amen.

What I'm about to tell you now should not be taken lightly. As a matter of fact this information is definitely necessary to know and believe.

Last, but certainly not least is faith. Faith in GOD to answer your Godly request is a major requirement. Here is where a lot of prayers are cancelled, lost, terminated or even trashed. If you would read and study the Word of GOD for yourself you would find a scripture: **Hebrews 11:1**, that says;

1) Now faith is the substance of things hoped for, the evidence of things not seen.

Just in case you don't understand this scripture, let me explain it to you in my own words. By the way, if you ever read and study the Word of GOD and don't get a clear understanding, or have a hard time understanding, you should stop and ask GOD to give you a clear understanding of His Word. He will give it give it to you because He wants you to understand. The Word of GOD was given to us by GOD for our benefit. How can we benefit from it, if we don't understand it?

Now back to the scripture on faith. The first half of this scripture refers to faith, your faith or true faith as a substance. I'll use the example of a simple product that we've all used at one time or another to illustrate what and how important faith is. The product I've chosen to use is glue. Would you get the picture if I said that your faith should be applied to your prayers like glue?

It could either be super glue or even crazy glue, as long as it holds your prayers together. Just as weak glue fails to hold two parts together, weak faith also fails to hold your prayers together.

In the Word of GOD, faith is the focus of the 11th Chapter of Hebrews. This chapter gives the names and actions, or acts of faith, of several individuals. These individuals are referred to as the Elders, whom because of their acts of faith obtained a good report.

There is even a scripture that tells you exactly how important your faith is to GOD. **Hebrews 11:6;**

6) But without faith it is impossible to please him: for he that cometh to God must believe that he is, and that he is a rewarder of them that diligently seek him.

I believe that GOD through the gift of the Holy Spirit has blessed me with faith, trust and belief in Him. When I go to GOD in prayer to ask for whatsoever I may want or need, I apply all these Words that I have mentioned so far in this chapter. I don't stop there because I want my faith to be strong.

How does a person's faith become strong? You would know this if you were reading and studying the Word of GOD. GOD is a true and wise GOD. He tells us all we need to know in His Word. We have to read and study His Word to hear what He has to say.

Here is what the Word of God has to say about where faith comes from. **Romans 10:17** says this;

17) So then faith cometh by hearing, and hearing by the word of God.

This is GOD's way of telling us that we need to hear His Word preached in church, in Bible studies with others and certainly we are to read and study the Word of GOD for ourselves. We need to testify as well as hear testimonies from others as to how GOD has blessed us and them, how he has given to us the things whatsoever we have asked of Him.

These are the things that will help strengthen your faith and the faith of others. Word of caution!!! Do not allow your faith to be regulated by your five senses. That's not where faith is. Our five senses were given to us to help us deal with the natural world around us. Faith is found in our spirits.

Pay close attention to this scenario. If you were to get hired on a job today and were told that you would get paid in two weeks you would report to work everyday. Then in two weeks you would expect your paycheck, right? Well, try this on for size. What if you didn't get paid? There is an expression found in the Old Testament which describes what some people did when they got angry. They rent, (tore up) their clothes.

But seriously back to the job situation. Your faith, trust and belief in what the employer told you have been received by your natural senses, you heard it. Then you received it in your spirit, you believed it. That's when your faith was born. Enough faith for you to report to work every morning, and when you didn't get paid, enough faith for you to get angry, tear up your clothes or maybe something else.

People of the Old Testament tore up their clothes, so be careful when you get angry. Smile.

Now do you see how faith works? Hold on a minute, the scripture on faith had two parts. The second part said that faith was also; the evidence of things not seen.

In order to gain a better understanding of this part of the scripture, I suggest that you substitute the word evidence with the word proof. As we substitute the word evidence with the word proof, we can now see how GOD Himself will receive your faith.

For example, in the natural world, evidence is most commonly seen and heard in the legal profession. In crimes, the weapon used or the monies confiscated is the evidence that will be presented to the jury as proof that a crime has been committed. Add to that the fact that it was found in your possession, or even having your fingerprints on it, tell of a situation that is not in your favor. In short, you will most likely be found guilty.

On the other hand, in the spiritual world of GOD, He views your faith as evidence or proof. Not enough or weak wavering faith will not speak on your behalf but good strong faith will testify before GOD that you are truly guilty, guilty of believing in Him and His promises.

All Rise!! Now, that your faith has been labeled as evidence, not against you, but for you. It can now be seen as proof that you have whatsoever you have asked of GOD right then, even before you see it. Remember the Word of GOD said; the evidence of things <u>not</u> seen.

That's why the title of this chapter asks the question; Seeing is Believing? The answer is no. Not when you have true faith in GOD. It's the exact opposite; **Believing is Seeing!** Amen?

Chapter #3

Everything Shiny, Ain't Gold

You are going to love this chapter. With the help of the Holy Spirit I will attempt to point out to you the difference between what has real lasting value and what doesn't.

Before I begin lets have a word of prayer.

Heavenly Father, please bless me, the writer, and the person who reads this chapter to fully understand the importance of knowing the difference between things that look good and catch the eye, but are of no real value, as opposed to those things that you have told us in your Word that you consider valuable. I ask this in the name of Jesus Christ. Amen.

I tried my best to remember to first time I ever heard the expression; "Everything Shiny, Ain't Gold". I can't seem to remember who said it or when I first heard it but it has definitely stuck in my mind and spirit ever since. Even though I can't recall who said it or where I heard it, I can still sense that it came to me as an eye opener, or if you will, a revelation.

I do remember this though, I agreed with whoever said it. It's as if I knew exactly what it meant with no doubts. I also believe the person who told me this was elderly and certainly wise. Some times, I view it as a sort of warning of things not to place a lot of value, energy, emotion, time or even thought into. As this thing, whatever it maybe, is not worth the effort of pursuing it, much less, obtaining it. I hope your still with me.

We live in a world with a kind of circus evince! A thousand and one attractions!!! Each one of them as eye catching as the Forth of July celebration or just as shiny as a new penny, bicycle, or for us grown up kids, a new car.

Do you know how a small child reacts to a brand new penny? If given a choice between a shiny new penny or any new coin and a dollar, the child will most likely choose the coin. Why? You guessed it, it's shiny.

How about this, the brand new bicycle? Back in my early years I had a bicycle. It had real working headlights, colorful streamers hanging from the handlebar and a seat over the back wheel for a friend to hitch a ride. It was really something. As nice and pretty as it was, it eventually lost its appeal. Over time the bright red paint faded. The headlights rusted out and I started to grow up. Not to mention a time or two it cost me some skin. Ouch!

As I grew older I bought a car, used. I gave it the best care that I could. I fed it, gasoline. I clothed it, new paint. I bought it new shoes, tires. I even bathed it. I was good to it but it always wanted something. It was never satisfied. It kept asking, no, begging, no, demanding more and more of my money and time. This thing, this shiny thing, as it turned out was not gold.

Now we come to the real deal, Gold; one of the most precious of all metals, something to be desired by men and woman alike. People have wasted their entire lives looking for it. Some have lost their lives in pursuit of it. It has been bought, sold, given and stolen. What's so special about it? Listen to this. It shines! Its appeal is in its glow. However it looses value from one moment to the next. Sure besides being worn as a form of jewelry it has some industrial applications, but even with that, the truth is, it's just a shiny piece of metal.

I have brought all of this to your attention so that you will search for something much more valuable. Something that the Almighty GOD values.

Through out this book I will remind you, ask you, even beg you to read and study the Word of GOD for yourself. If and when you do, GOD Himself, through His Word will bless you with wisdom, knowledge and understanding. His wisdom will tell you not to pursue the riches of this world, gold. His knowledge will teach you why, it holds no real value. By His understanding, you will know that regardless of how much of the world riches you obtain, you won't be able to take it with you and it certainly cannot save you.

When it comes to obtaining the riches, or storing up the treasures of this world, GOD in His Word, tells us the truth. **Matthew 6:19**;

19) Lay not up for yourselves treasures upon the earth, where moth and rust doth corrupt, and where thieves break through and steal:

Also, GOD in His Word, continues to explain to us where we should store up our treasures. **Verse 20** says;

20) But lay up for yourselves treasures in heaven, where neither moth nor rust doth corrupt, and where thieves do not break through nor steal:

Now these scriptures, I believe, don't mean that we shouldn't try to be successful. I'm sure GOD wants us to prosper. The truth that GOD wants us to understand is found in **Matthew 16:26**;

26) For what is a man profited, if he shall gain the whole world, and lose his own soul? or what shall a man give in exchange for his soul?

In this next verse of scripture, the Word of GOD reveals more truth. Again, from the book of **Matthew 6: 21**;

21) For where your treasure is, there will your heart be also.

I'm sure you know that there are people whose lives are totally rapped up in their worldly riches or treasures. In the scripture you just read (**verse 21**), GOD tells us that, where your treasures are, that's where your heart is.

The heart of a person can be used, in a descriptive sense to make a statement about them. Some people are described as being heartless, which is cruel or mean. Others are referred to as having a heart of gold, caring or giving. So you see the kind of heart a person has says a lot about that person's character.

In the Word of GOD we can also find a scripture in which a rich man is being used as an example. **Luke 12:16 to 21**says;

16) And he spake a parable unto them, saying, The ground of a certain rich man brought forth plentifully:

17) And he thought within himself, saying, What shall I do, because I have no room where to bestow my fruits?

18) And he said, This will I do: I will pull down my barns, and build greater; and there will I bestow all my fruits and my goods.

19) And I will say to my soul, soul, thou hast much goods laid up for many years; take thine ease, eat, drink, and be merry.

20) But GOD said unto him, thou fool, this night thy soul shall be required of thee: then whose shall those things be, which thou hast, provided?

21) So is he that layeth up treasures for himself, and is not rich toward GOD.

What the Word of God is saying here is very important to us and to GOD. He is saying in no uncertain terms that a person is a fool for laying up worldly treasures, especially selfishly. He also tells us what is real wealth or treasure.

Reading and studying the Word of God for yourself is a good way to get to know GOD. GOD tells us how He feels about everything under the Sun.

In His Word He tells us that the rich man referred to in **Luke 12:16 to 21**; had an abundance of this worlds wealth. He had so much he didn't even know what to do with it. This man decided to tear down his old barns and build larger new ones to hoard his blessings. Then he could just sit back and take it easy. Eat, Drink and be Merry. I guess he thought he had it going on.

He could not have been more wrong. I believe that GOD was even angry at his selfish attitude, thinking only of himself. Not taking into consideration who had blessed him with the bountiful treasures he now wanted to store up for himself. Shame on you!

I tell my family and friends this; GOD did not bless you so that you can tell everybody how blessed you are: He blessed you to be a blessing to someone else!

In closer observation, it would appear that this rich man valued his relationship with his treasures more than he did a rich relationship with GOD. While he was busy tearing down his old barns and building new ones, he should have been doing the kind of things that GOD values, therefore storing up treasures in heaven.

Do you know how to store up treasures in heaven? Well then, let me ask you this. Have you ever helped a stranger? Have you done good deeds, not only to your friends, but your enemies as well? Have you given your time and or money in the service of others? Have you given back to GOD the first and best part of your income, paying tithes? Have you given your Love?

Brothers and Sisters, these are the kinds of things that GOD considers as treasures. These are the kinds of things, treasures, that GOD Almighty will see you do and be pleased. GOD will not forget these things. In this way you are storing up treasures in heaven.

Believe me when I tell you this. These things go ahead of you, because we all know we can't take anything with us. Not even one hand full of gold. As if GOD needed our small hand full of gold.

If you were to read and study the Word of GOD for yourself, you would find that gold, pure gold, is something that GOD has plenty of. In fact, GOD reveals to us in His Word that in the city of New Jerusalem, the street is pure gold. **Revelation 21:21** says;

21) And the twelve gates were twelve pearls; every several gate was of one pearl: and the street of the city was pure gold, as it were transparent glass.

Can you imagine that? Don't you want to see it? Don't you want to live in it? Want to know how to get there? You may not realize it but we have a map. This map is none other than the Word of GOD. If you were to read and study the Word of GOD for yourself and then follow its directions, you would not get lost.

I urge you not to take directions from just anyone. Some people are really lost but they don't know it. They have been given the wrong directions by someone else who was lost. Please don't fall victim to this cycle of blind leading the blind. Take my sincere advice. Read and study the Word of GOD for yourself.

I hope that you have enjoyed this chapter. I know that I have given you a lot of information to absorb. You will do well if you remember these two things. Take some time each day to read and study the Word of GOD and **Everything Shiny, Ain't Gold.**

Chapter #4

Sin and Shame, Identical Twins

Reading and studying the Word of GOD has blessed me, by way of the Holy Spirit, to realize and recognize, that Sin and Shame are directly related to one another. Even to the point that I see them as Identical Twins. As we continue through this chapter we will examine first of all what Sin is and later, what it ain't.

Right away my mind made some quick and accurate assessments of the situation. My mind easily fell on some of the things that I have done in my life that fall into the category of Sin.

Let's face it, no one is without Sin. By the way I've already taken my dirty laundry to get washed so I won't be airing any of them here. I said that because other people's dirty laundry or sins seem to be more interesting to us than our own. I wonder why that is?

Anyhow, according to the Word of GOD in **Romans 3:23**;

23) For all have sinned, and come short of the glory of God;

As I mentioned in a previous chapter, GOD is true and wise. In his love, compassion and mercy, GOD has given to us, in His Word, the answers to all of our problems, even sin.

This is just another reason for you to read and study the Word of GOD for yourself. The Word of GOD tells us exactly what sin is, the effects of sin and how to be forgiven our sins. GOD, in His wisdom even took the time to tell us how to avoid sin.

I make it a practice to always ask for forgiveness of the sins I commit in thought, in act, in word or deed. I'm not taking any chances with sin.

Now that I've mentioned what I do, let me tell you what the Word of GOD has to say about receiving forgiveness of sin. In **1st John 1:9**, the Word of GOD says;

9) If we confess our sins, he is faithful and just to forgive us our sins, and to cleanse us from all unrighteousness.

To me Brothers and Sisters this is a good thing, a real good thing. I say this because sin is what separates us from GOD. Surely you can see by His Word that GOD is good to us. In His Word you will come to know all about His goodness and mercy. GOD knows more about us than we will ever know about ourselves. He not only knows when we sin, He even knows before we sin.

Sin, Brothers and Sisters is nothing new. Sin has been around ever since the days of Adam and Eve. In fact, this is actually when to first sin took place. I'm sure most of us have heard the story of Adam and Eve. Let's take a closer look at the very first sin ever committed.

The place, Eden, a beautiful garden, the sin, disobedience! I'll explain; not doing what the Almighty GOD said to do or doing what He said not to do: is exactly the same thing, Disobedience.

If you read and study the Word of GOD, you'll find that after Adam and Eve had sinned or were disobedient, to make a long story short; they hid themselves.

In **Genesis 3:9 and 10**, scripture says;

9) And the Lord God called unto Adam, and said unto him, where art thou?

10) And he said, I heard thy voice in the garden, and I was afraid, because I was naked; and I hid myself.

Adam and Eve wouldn't have had any idea that they were naked if they had not sinned or been disobedient. Adam clearly stated that he was afraid and with good reason. What's interesting is that they hid.

Here is where I want to introduce you to Sin's twin sister, Shame. Hello my name is Shame and I am always with my sister, Sin. We are identical twins but we're not the same. We hang out together, we even double date, but we each have a different nature.

If we were bank robbers, my sister Sin would lead the way in and I Shame; would lead the way out. When you set your heart on something that's not yours, the twins are right there. One says go and the other says come.

These two sisters can be very influential in a person's life, especially if they don't know that they are always together. What makes it so bad is that they are not friends of mankind. They love to trick us and then sit back and laugh at us. One of them says to the other, you say this and I'll say that.

They are really out to convince us that we can get away with our acts of disobedience.

They love to tell us things like, GOD won't know, your wife, your husband, your boss, even your congregation, won't know. Yea right! That's the trap. Don't believe me? Then take a look at this.

Do you remember this well known televangelist whom confessed to a sin, (and I won't go into detail), on national television? Here's a hint. The poor man had tears in his eyes. Did you see it? Did you notice the twins? I did, they were standing there, one on each side of him. Both of them grinning and waving as if they had won first place on Star Search or American Idol.

Millions of people saw that broadcast but I'll bet not many people saw the twins, Sin and Shame. My heart went out to this man. I really felt sorry for him. Maybe he didn't know that Sin had a twin.

There was a time, before I started to read and study the word of GOD, that I didn't know that Sin had a twin. It was right after I had committed a terrible sin that, Sin introduced me to Shame. I'm glad I met them in a way because now I know them. I've seen the beauty of their ugly faces, especially when I looked into the mirror. I literally wanted to rent my clothes.

Believe it or not, the twins, Sin and Shame, are as people say, are as old as Methuselah, I say older. From Adam and Eve, all through history, they have been together.

In a more recent high profile situation, they even paid a visit to one our dear presidents. When he addressed the nation and confessed to his wrong doing, or sin, the twins were right there. Get this, he wasn't the only one affected by the twins, M. L. also.

The actual count of those affected is unimaginable. So you see, Sin and Shame, as old as they are, have not changed a bit. They are still as evil as they were in the days of Adam and Eve.

In the beginning of this chapter I made a statement, "let's examine first what sin is and later, what it ain't". I've told you basically what sin is; Disobedience to GOD!

Now pay very close attention to what sin ain't. Are you ready? Hold on, this may come as a shock to some of you. Here it is.

Reading and Studying the Word of GOD for yourself, Is Not a Sin! Got it? GOOD.

In conclusion, I want to leave you with this. The story of Adam and Eve had another character referred to as a serpent. This serpent is a representation of Satan, the Father of Lies.

Not only is he the Father of Lies, he is also the father of; you guessed it, Sin and Shame. He's like a father desperately trying to find husbands for his daughters, or for you females, friends for them. He'll invite you over to meet them. He'll describe them as being nice, sweet and beautiful. What he won't tell you is that there names are Sin and Shame.

Now that I have told you about the twins, hopefully you won't want to meet them and certainly not go out with them. For you sisters, don't even try to become their friends.

Just in case you do decide to hang out with **Sin**, she will surely introduce you to her twin sister **Shame.** Let the reader beware.

Chapter #5

Law or Grace

As in all the chapters of this book, I have asked GOD to bless me, by way of the Holy Spirit, to be able to deliver to you a message that is both clear and concise. I'm sure by now you have received a message from this book that is not hidden, or as modern technology would say, subliminal, but is plain, straight forward, and to the point. Just in case you have missed it, here it is again.

Please read and study the Word of GOD for yourself!

This chapter is about choices, or should I say, a choice. What I'm referring to is the difference between the Law, which was given to Moses in the Old Testament and Grace, which we are afforded through faith in our Lord and Savior, Jesus Christ.

I will begin by telling you about the Laws that were given to Moses by the Almighty GOD. As I read and studied the Word of GOD, I noticed that

GOD made a change in the way things were to be done. Some people speak of GOD as unyielding, unchanging; evidently they haven't read the Bible. The very title of this chapter tells of a change that the Almighty GOD made; a major change. In other words, GOD doesn't change, but he makes changes.

Once upon a time and this is no fairy tale. In the Old Testament, our GOD; the GOD of Abraham, Isaac and Jacob, decided He would choose a certain people for Himself. These people were called the Children of Israel. They lived in Egypt under the rule of Pharaoh, the King of Egypt, in slavery. The scriptures tell us that they were treated harshly. **Exodus 1:13 and 14** says;

13) And the Egyptians made the children of Israel to serve with rigour:

14) And they made their lives bitter with hard bondage, in morter, and in brick, and in all manner of service in the field: all their service, wherein they made them serve, was with rigour.

You can tell that being a slave to the Egyptians was not a good thing. However, GOD had a plan. This is where Moses comes in at.

I will only give you the highlights here because I want you to read and study the Word of GOD for yourself.

GOD heard the moaning, groaning and prayers of the Children of Israel. In fact, He chose Moses to go to Pharaoh and demand; "Let my people go! GOD had much compassion for the Children of Israel. In **Exodus 6: verses 7 and 8**, God revealed His plan for them.

7) And I will take you to me for a people, and I will be to you a God: and ye shall know that I am the Lord your God, which bringeth you out from under the burdens of the Egyptians.

8) And I will bring you in unto the land, concerning the which I did swear to give it to Abraham, to Isaac, and to Jacob; and will give it you for an heritage: I am the Lord.

Moses, being chosen of GOD to be the leader of His people, led the Children of Israel out of Egypt. The Children of Israel were much like the people of the world today. They were disobedient, stubborn and they complained all the time.

According to the Word of GOD, two months after the Children of Israel, or Israelites, left Egypt, they came to the Sinai desert. The Israelites then set up camp at the foot of Mount Sinai.

From the Word of GOD we find that this is where the Almighty GOD gave Moses the Ten Commandments. GOD was very clear in His commandments to the Israelites. GOD didn't leave anything to chance. He was careful to cover everything under the Sun that He wanted them to do or not to do.

GOD gave, and you can read these Laws in detail, in the book of Exodus. There were General Rules for Worship, Laws concerning the treatment of Slaves, Laws concerning Injury to People, Laws concerning Property, not to mention, Laws for Living as Gods Holy People and many more.

Actually, the Ten Commandments were a base for the Laws GOD intended the Israelites to live by. What GOD said, and this is still true today, He means.

During this time, to be disobedient to GOD could mean death, or at the least, banishment from the Israelite camp. Because of GOD's love, compassion and mercy, He also placed into the Law a sort of payment plan for when a person broke the Law.

These were an exact set of sacrifices and offerings for the people's disobedience, intentional or unintentional. GOD did not play. The only way to please GOD in those days was to follow the Law to the letter.

All of the things I just told you about are written in the Word of GOD, the Bible, and I haven't even scratched the surface. When I first read these things the Holy Spirit brought me to a deeper appreciation of GOD's love and mercy. Thank you Lord Jesus!

Can you imagine what it was like to live under the Law? I'm not passing judgment on GOD's way of doing things, no never.

GOD is GOD, all by Himself. He can most certainly do anything He pleases. He is the creator. In other words, we are His possessions. We really don't have a right to complain. We were created by Him for His purpose and will. Question, "Does the pot ask the potter; what are you making?

As I mentioned before, in the Old Testament, GOD knew people would sin. That's why he gave them specific things to do in order to be forgiven. People had to sacrifice bulls, lambs, birds and other things. Everything was brought to the priest, Aaron, Moses' brother, and his sons. No one else could even approach GOD to ask forgiveness or anything else. I told you in the beginning of this chapter that GOD doesn't change, but He makes changes.

Now we come to the New Testament. Here is where we are introduced to John the Baptist, the Twelve Disciples and best of all, our Lord and Savior Jesus Christ.

The coming of our Lord and Savior Jesus Christ was a major change in our relationship with GOD, a change that is based on the grace of GOD and not on the ability of man to follow the Laws that were given to Moses. **John 1:17** tells us;

17) For the law was given by Moses, but grace and truth came by Jesus Christ.

What this means is that through a sincere belief in Jesus Christ we have grace and as the song says; Amazing Grace! This grace that is given, gives each and everyone of us the opportunity to be saved from the wrath of GOD's anger. Through grace we have freedom.

It is not necessary for us to make sacrifices or offerings to GOD in return for His forgiveness of our sins.

Our Lord and Savior Jesus Christ was a one time sacrifice. When His precious blood was shed on the Cross of Calvary, it covered all of the sins of the entire world, everyone, and everywhere. Those of us who call on his Holy and Righteous name receive His grace.

When we, as the scriptures say in **Romans 3:23**;

23) For all have sinned and come short of the glory of GOD;

The grace of our Lord and Savior Jesus Christ is right there. The Word of GOD also tells us in the book of **2ⁿᵈ Corinthians 12:9** that,

9) And he said unto me, My grace is sufficient for thee: for my strength is made perfect in weakness. Most gladly therefore will I rather glory in my infirmities, that the power of Christ may rest upon me.

I don't know about you, but that's what I call amazing. When you read and study the Word of GOD for yourself and find out about GOD's infinite wisdom, knowledge, understanding, mercy, compassion, love and grace, you too will be amazed.

You will want to serve Him, praise Him, thank Him, worship Him, tell others about Him and maybe even write a book encouraging people to read and study His Word. Hey it could happen!

Once again I remind you that this chapter is about choices or should I say a choice. GOD has given us a free will. He did not create us to be robots. We are His creation and yes He really does love us, but we have to choose to accept and receive His love, forgiveness and Word.

I believe that GOD has blessed me through the Holy Spirit with the words of this book. To Him I give all the glory, honor and the praise.

The transition from Old Testament to the New Testament was one of utmost importances. Our Lord and Savior, Jesus Christ brought to us something that the Laws of Moses could not.

The Word of GOD says in the book of **Acts 13:38 and 39,**

> **38) Be it known unto you therefore, men and brethren that through this man is preached unto you the forgiveness of sins:**

> **39) And by him all that believe are justified from all things, from which ye could not be justified by the law of Moses.**

Do you see the difference between the Law and Grace? Believe me when I tell you this, there are people, even men of GOD, who like to tell others of a way to serve GOD that is based on the Law.

Before ending this chapter I want to show again why it is so important for you to read and study the Word of GOD for yourself.

The scriptures that I am about to refer to are not to be taken lightly. Hopefully, you will be able to identify your choices and make an intelligent and well informed decision.

Read these scriptures as many times you need to, I want you to fully understand them. I'm sure its GOD's intentions that we read and receive His Word.

In the Word of GOD, the word circumcised is used to identify those who try to live by the Law. In the book of **Galatians 5:1 thru 6**, these Words are recorded.

1) **Stand fast therefore in the liberty wherewith Christ hath made us free, and be not entangled again with the yoke of bondage.**

2) Behold, I Paul say unto you, that if ye be circumcised, Christ shall profit you nothing.

3) For I testify again to every man that is circumcised, that he is a debtor to do the whole law.

4) Christ is become of no effect unto you, whosoever of you are justified by the law; ye are fallen from grace.

5) For we through the Spirit wait for the hope of righteousness by faith.

6) For in Jesus neither circumcision availeth anything, nor uncircumcision; but faith which worketh by love.

Brothers and Sisters because of the grace of our Lord and Savior Jesus Christ, we have freedom, but we are not to take advantage of this freedom. I wish to offer just two more scriptures I believe will be helpful to you in your understanding of the freedom or liberty afforded us through faith in Jesus Christ.

Once again from the book of Galatians **5**th **Chapter, 13**th **and 14**th, verses;

13) For brethren, ye have been called unto liberty; only use not liberty for an occasion to the flesh, but by love serve one another.

14) For all the law is fulfilled in one word, even in this; Thou shalt love thy neighbor as thyself.

Well there you have it, the GOD's honest truth. Question is, how do you want to live? By the **Law or Grace?**

Chapter #6

Separation Between Church and State

Now you've gone and done it! That's right, I'm accusing you! I know what you're thinking. What exactly did you do? There will be no doubt in your mind by the time you get to the end of this chapter.

Before I continue to accuse you, let's pause while I ask GOD Almighty to bless me with the words to say, that will inspire or maybe even dare you to stand up for the Christian values, concepts and ideals, that one as precious as our Lord and Savior, Jesus Christ, was crucified so many could be free. It is in the name of Jesus Christ, that I ask, Amen.

Where was I? Oh yea! So you're just going to sit there and act as if you don't know what I'm talking about. I'm angry to say the least. You betrayed me. You are responsible for some, if not all, that has happened to me. Why? How could you? Didn't you know? Couldn't you see it coming? You hurt me so bad. I thought you loved me! Oh I get it, you were too busy. You weren't paying attention.

He slipped into the door and hid right in front of you. Of course you saw him but you didn't even question him. You allowed him to stay and never knew what he had planned.

He did this ugly thing right in front of you and you thought nothing of it. He used you to cheat me, to steal from me, to destroy me; and you have the nerve to ask me, what did I do? Well I'll tell you what you did. Nothing, absolutely nothing!

The worst thing you could have possibly done was nothing. To you maybe what you didn't do was not a big deal. If you had rent your clothes, I wouldn't have torn mine. Our ancestors made it clear. What part did you not understand? Did you think they were crazy?

No, they were blessed. They saw the source and pointed to it for you to see. You have no excuses. What can you say? Aren't you ashamed? Well you should be; I am.

All of what I have just said expresses the way I feel about the title of this chapter, Separation Between Church and State. The part of this rather controversial subject that has really got me in a sour mood is the removal of prayers from our public schools.

The impact that this has had on our great nation can be seen in many ways. I find it hard to believe at times, but when I read and study the Word of GOD, I also find that there is nothing new under the Sun. This has happened before somewhere in human history, it was just called by a different name.

To be totally honest with you, I believe GOD has chosen this particular topic to challenge you. What I'm talking about is backing down, submitting, not fighting back, and throwing in the towel.

In our society, we, the Christians, commit any one of these acts which could be considered as crimes and yes we still do it. We carelessly look the other way while the enemy advances on our front. We lock ourselves in our homes, cars and churches; comfortable and yet so unaware. My friends this is what the enemy uses against us. When we take a step back, the enemy takes a step forward.

The word enemy is used in the Word of GOD to describe none other than Satan. This also implies that a battle has ensued and that war is at hand. The battle line is drawn. We as Christians are no doubt on the winning team because GOD Almighty is on our side. Hallelujah!

In the book of **Exodus, chapter 17**, we can read about how GOD brings a victory against an enemy of the Israelites, the Amalekites. The Word of GOD also tells us what GOD had in store for the enemy in the future. The following scriptures define the actions of GOD and the importance of man (Christians) to hold up a banner for GOD. The banner is represented by the staff of Moses or in other words, the Rod of GOD.

Exodus 17:8 thru 16 reads;

8) Them came Amalek, and fought with Israel in Rephidim.

9) And Moses said unto Joshua, choose us out men, and go out, fight with Amalek: to morrow I will stand on the top of the hill with the rod of God in mine hand.

10) So Joshua did as Moses had said to him, and fought with Amalek: and Moses, Aaron and Hur went up to the top of the hill.

11) and it came to pass, when Moses held up his hand, that Israel prevailed.

12) But Moses' hands were heavy, and they took a stone, and put it under him, and he sat thereon; and Aaron and Hur stayed up his hands, the one on the one side, and the other on the other side; and his hands were steady until the going down of the sun.

13) And Joshua discomforted Amalek and his people with the edge of the sword.

14) And the lord said unto Moses, write this for a memorial in a book, and rehearse it in the ears of Joshua: for I will utterly put out the remembrance of Amalek from under heaven.

15) And Moses built an alter, and called the name of it Jehovah-nissi.

16) For he said, Because the Lord has sworn that the Lord will have war Amalek from generation to generation.

In these scriptures, it may be somewhat difficult to completely grasp all that is being said. The understanding that I received is that, the Staff of Moses, or as the scripture says; the Rod of God, was the deciding factor in the outcome of the battle between the Israelites and the Amalekites.

Verse 11 clearly states that when Moses held up his hand (the rod of God), the Israelites prevailed. We can surmise that when he lowered the rod of God the Amalekites or enemy prevailed. There is a definite message in this scripture. This scripture tells us that when GOD is on your side you just can't loose. We are also being told that we must do our part, no matter what.

Moses truly understood this concept and did the best he could to continue to hold up the rod of GOD. It's not easy to hold up a pencil for an extended period of time, much less, a rod or staff. In fact we learn that Moses became weary, his hands became heavy. Thanks to Aaron and Hur, he had help. These men took a stand for GOD and were victorious. Amen!

At the setting of the Sun, the Amalekites, or the enemy, was defeated. The last part of this story tells us that GOD, the Lord, thought this victory was worthy of recording (writing) as well as being told over and over again (rehearsed) into the ears of Joshua (the people).

We are also being told that the Lord has sworn to have war with Amalek or the enemy from generation to generation. Here is where GOD is telling us that the war between His people, Christians, and the enemy is not over with the winning of this one battle.

To me the words; from generation to generation, speak for themselves.

When you read and study the Word of GOD, you'll find many scriptures that teach and inspire us to stand up for GOD and in return, He will most certainly stand up for us.

Romans 10:11 says;

11) For this scripture saith, WHOSOEVER BELIEVETH ON HIM SHALL NOT BE ASHAMED.

To me this is GOD's guarantee.

As I have mentioned in all of the preceding chapters it is very important that we read and study the Word of GOD. In the first part of this chapter I made mention of the fact that I was a bit angered, sour, about the removal of prayer from our public schools.

When we, the Christians of today, lower our modern day staffs and rods of GOD, our enemy Satan is able to advance on our front. Do you think it was GOD's idea to remove prayer from our public schools? Of course not!

When I read and study the Word of GOD I find that we are encouraged to pray. **1ˢᵗ Thessalonians 5:17** says,

17) Pray without ceasing.

With all of the evil in this world, we need to read and study the Word of GOD daily as well as pray daily. We can't afford to become too relaxed and let our guards down. Remember, from generation to generation, the war is not over yet.

I want you, to encourage others not only to read and study the Word of GOD, but to also take a stand for GOD. There are Christians in every area of life. We are in the schools, courtrooms, and politics. In fact these are just a few of the battlefields. We need to take on the attitude of a true soldier. We need to fight the enemy toe to toe and not back down one bit.

When it was suggested that prayer be removed from public schools we should have held up the Rod of GOD and defeated our enemy.

We are a nation that had a message given to us that rings as clear as the Liberty Bell. Want to know what this message is? No, I'm not going to say read and study the Word of GOD. There are four more chapters in this book and I plan to mention that plenty of times.

What I want to say or better yet show you can be found in your own pockets. Here is where you get a chance to interact with the message of this chapter. Take a coin or any denomination of cash from your pocket or purse. Study it carefully.

Do you see it? It's right there! Allow me to read it to you. IN GOD WE TRUST. Wow! Where did that come from? Who could have put that there? It's my guess that GOD did through the Holy Spirit as a reminder for us. This also tells me something about our forefathers; you know the one who wrote; fourscore and seven years ago . . .

These men most definitely read and studied the Word of GOD. They not only read and studied it, they also believed it. Have we gotten so comfortable and relaxed that we have forgotten who we are? We are one nation under GOD!

The Word of GOD has many scriptures about placing trust in GOD. Here is one I want you to write on the tablet of your heart.

Proverbs 3:5;

5) Trust in the Lord with all your heart; and lean not to thine own understanding.

With so much emphasis being placed on trusting GOD, it's hard to believe that we allowed prayer to be removed from our public schools.

Look at what's happening in our schools today. Can't you see how our dear children are suffering from spiritual neglect? Do you know that there are children that don't attend church or hear any other forms of teachings about GOD? The same GOD, who asked us to place all of our trust in Him!

That they are part of a country where the founders or forefathers stated we should trust in GOD! Are you beginning to understand how vitally important it is for you to read and study the Word of GOD? One more good reason is so that we can teach our children about GOD.

I am going to leave from the original writings of this manuscript to interject some scriptures that the Lord has laid on my heart about what will happen to a person who refuses to retain GOD in their knowledge. From the book of **Romans, Chapter 1, verses 28 thru 30;**

28) And even as they did not like to retain God in their knowledge, God gave them over to a reprobate mind, to do those things which are not convenient;

29) Being filled with all unrighteousness, fornication, wickedness, covetousness, maliciousness; full of envy, murder, debate, deceit, malignity; whisperers,

30) Backbiters, haters of God, despiteful, proud, boasters, inventors of evil things, disobedient to parents,

I had better stop here so that you can read and study the rest for yourselves.

In closing I want to ask you this. Do we send our children out into the world without some kind of protection? When it's cold outside we tell them to put on a coat. When it rains, we say put a hat on your head. We feed them, we clothe them and we do our best to take care of them.

Let's give them something that will really help them. Let's tell them about GOD! Let's allow GOD Himself to lead and guide them. The Word of GOD says its man who plants the seed but its GOD who makes it grow. Plant the seed of the Word of GOD in your child's life. Do it because I know you love them.

One final point I want to make in this chapter is this. When we start to allow non-believers to lead us, we had better watch out. Theses people are spiritually blind! We would do just as good if we were to be led around by a seeing-eye-dog!

I hope that this chapter has really stirred you up. I'm reminded of an old time gospel song entitled; Catch on Fire! I really do wish that your soul would catch on fire, burning with the Holy Ghost.

Again, please read and study the Word of GOD. I believe that GOD will show you, too, that the **Separation Between Church and State,** was not His idea.

Chapter #7

Pay the Cost, to be the Boss

Heavenly and merciful Father, I want to thank you and praise you for all of the many wonderful blessings that you have bestowed upon me. Most of all I want to thank you for your love. A love so deep, that you sent your only begotten Son, Jesus Christ, to suffer and die on the Cross at Calvary, not only for my sins but for the sins of the world. Heavenly Father I praise you, I glorify your holy and righteous name. I say HALLELUHAH, even Glory HALLELHAH to your praise. I humbly ask that you continue to lead and guide me through your Holy Spirit, that in this chapter you bless me with the words to say that removes any and all doubt as to who has truly paid the cost to be the boss. I ask this in the name of Jesus Christ. Amen.

This like all of the chapters in this book has a definite purpose in mind. However, the overall purpose of this book is to encourage you, the reader, to read and study the Word of GOD so that certain issues in our lives and society can be better understood. To bring an awareness of what has been given us by GOD, in His Word, also expose the myths and untruths that so many people fall victim to.

So far as you have read this book I have tried to uncover some of the lies that our common enemy, Satan, has told to the people of this world to casually look upon as things that really don't matter. We can be sure of this one thing, Satan is a liar! If Satan is behind it then his motives are the same, to steal, kill and destroy.

The truth is that every word, every practice, every idea and every belief that does not line up with the Word of GOD, put plain and simple, is a lie. One of the best ways of finding out the truths of GOD is by reading and studying His Word.

The best way to fall victim to the lies of Satan is to believe and conform to the beliefs and practices of the world. In the Word of GOD, **1**[st] **Peter, Chapter 2, verse 9** speaks another clear message to us.

> **9) But ye are a chosen generation, a royal priesthood, an holy nation, a peculiar people; that ye should shew forth the praises of him who hath called you out of darkness into his marvelous light.**

Here the Word of GOD makes mention of a calling out. Friends, God has truly called us out from the beliefs and practices of this world. We are being referred to as a chosen generation, a royal priesthood, etc.

We must read and study the Word of GOD and accept the truth! The marvelous light spoken of includes many things. The knowledge of GOD, the Grace of GOD, His Wisdom, His Love and His mercy; in other words its all good! I threw that in so that you would know that I have heard some of the sayings of the world.

The saying, "It's all good', no matter how catchy it is, can also be used to casually look upon the lies of Satan. When you read and study the Word of GOD, the Holy Spirit will show you and teach you what is truly, all good.

In the Word of GOD we can find warning after warning about Satan. Near the end of the first epistle of **Peter or 1ˢᵗ Peter 5:8** says;

8) Besober,bevigilant;becauseyouradversary the devil, as a roaring lion, walketh about, seeking whom he may devour.

We are being told that Satan is out there in the world looking for victims. He can't help it, it's his nature!

I am reminded of a story about a frog, a scorpion and a pond. In this story, the frog and the scorpion engage in a conversation about crossing the pond. The frog is a very good swimmer and knows it. On the other hand, the scorpion can't swim a lick and knows it.

As the story goes on, the scorpion asked the frog can he hitch a ride to the other side of the pond? The frog is apprehensive, to say the least and makes this comment; "O.K, but you know that if you sting me, we will both drown. The scorpion reassures the frog that he will not sting him and hops on his back. When the frog with the scorpion on his back swim to about the middle of the pond, you guessed it, the scorpion stings him. The poor frog cries out in despair; "Why did you do that, now both of us are going to die!

The scorpion simply said: "I couldn't help myself, it was in my nature".

This little story contains a big message. The poor frog fell victim to the lies of the scorpion just as people fall victim to the lies of Satan. The outcome is always the same. Not good at all. Just as it is in the nature of the scorpion to sting, it is also in the nature of Satan to kill, steal and destroy. When we don't read and study the Word of GOD, we set ourselves up to believe what's said and done in the world.

Believe it or not, the Word of GOD speaks of Satan as being the ruler of this world. Here is where I want to make a connection between the words ruler and boss.

When we hear the word ruler, we think of a person who is in control of a nation or group of people. When we hear the word boss, we usually associate it with the workplace. The person who is in charge is referred to as being the boss. This is indeed true as the boss can hire or fire you, for not working up to the company's standard.

Some of us work very long hard hours to impress our bosses as a means of obtaining a promotion or a raise. The person who we call boss has in some way been given authority over us. They have either achieved a higher level of education than ours or they have been on the job longer. Doing a good job themselves, have risen up through the company and based on their experience and abilities, been found worthy of the title boss.

These things can be looked upon as the price this person has paid to be the boss. However the cost, they did whatever they had to do, to pay it.

The words boss or ruler as you can see are really synonyms. Although they are two different words, they basically hold the same meaning. Let's cut to the chase.

If you are a person who accepts the beliefs and practices of this world and Satan is referred to as the ruler of this world, whom do you think is your boss?

Here is another question. What price has he paid? I believe he has been given a position of boss or ruler over all those that fall victim to his lies, the lies of the world.

Friends, I could write an entire book on the lies of Satan. Only by reading and studying the Word of GOD have I been led into the truth. I now have no doubts, none whatsoever, as to whom is my boss. I am also completely aware of the price that was paid by him.

The cost of my and your salvation was certainly not cheep. To fully understand this I had to read and study the Word of GOD for myself.

In the Word of GOD we can read all of the details of our Lord and Savior, Jesus Christ and the enormous price that He paid for us. In the four Gospels we find what had to come to pass in order for you and me to enjoy the benefits of GOD's grace and mercy.

In the books of Matthew, Mark, Luke and John, we are told of the suffering, shame, beatings, death and resurrection of our Lord and Savior Jesus Christ.

In the popular scripture **John 3:16** we are told of the ultimate price GOD Almighty paid for us and why. **John 3:16** says;

16) For GOD so loved the world, that he gave his only begotten Son, that whoever would believe in him should not perish, but have everlasting life.

Do you get the fullness of what is being said in this scripture? I'll use a few questions that will hopefully bring a depth to your understanding.

Do you have children? Would you or could you send anyone of your children to what you yourself knows is certain death? What if you only had one child to begin with?

Could or would you send the only child you have to a place where you know they would be beaten, slapped, spit on, cursed at, lied on, striped half-naked, nailed to a cross and then put on display for the whole world to see? Could you, would you? Would you allow these things to happen to you in a self sacrifice?

The word of GOD tells of how once in a while a person may sacrifice them self for a good person, but what about a murderer, rapist, thief, prostitute or plain old liar, you know, sinners?

To know that Jesus Christ went through all of the abuses that I mentioned, for all people, brings a new meaning to the word we casually use, Love. Here is what the Word of GOD has to say about it. **John 15:13** says;

13) Greater love has no man than this, that a man lay down his life for his friends.

Now that we have seen by the Word of GOD who has paid the cost there should be no doubt in our minds as to who should be the boss. I really want you to consider who, is your boss.

Are you working for GOD? Doing the things that he has asked us to do or are you doing the kinds of things that Satan wants you to do? Before you make the wrong assumption and continue to do whatever your little heart desires, you really need to start and continue to read and study the Word of GOD.

Remember, the Word of GOD said that there is no greater love, than the love He had for us that he laid down his life for his friends. I want you to see this and learn from it. His friends, get it? He said; "His Friends".

John 15:14 explains whom Jesus says are His friends.

14) Ye are my friends, if ye do whatsoever I command you.

Examine for yourself, those who are not your friends are called your enemies. So are those to Christ who don't heed the Words of GOD. How can you heed the Word of GOD if you don't know, hear or read and study the Word of GOD?

This is why I ask you all through this book to please, read and study the Word of GOD for yourself.

After reading this chapter there should not be any doubts in your mind. You should boldly go out and tell the world that you work for our Lord and Savior Jesus Christ. Why, because He has truly **Paid the Cost, to be the Boss.**

Chapter #8

Tricks of the Trade

As I always do, I will continue to. All I'm saying is that I always ask GOD to allow His Holy Spirit to bless me to write this book in Spirit and in Truth. Hear my prayer Heavenly Father and continue to grant me thy blessings. In the name of Jesus Christ, I ask, Amen.

This chapter, I hope and pray will bring insight, wisdom and a new understanding of these things that I refer to as being, Tricks of the Trade. I hope that I can stir you up as I endeavor to point out to you the tricks that Satan commonly uses against each and every one of us in everyday life. I want you to pay very close attention to these tricks and govern yourselves accordingly.

As I wrote the rough draft to this book I was told that some people may not like some of the things that I am saying. I thought to myself, with a smile, good. You see I'm not writing this book to please people. As you have probably noticed I write about issues that are important in our lives. It is very important that <u>we</u> read and study the Word of GOD.

I haven't shown you the scripture in which GOD Almighty tells us about His Word and the purpose of it. Well read and receive.

2nd Timothy, 3rd chapter and 16th verse says;

16) All scripture is given by inspiration of God, and is profitable for doctrine, for reproof, for correction, for instruction in righteousness:

There are many scriptures that have been given to show us the benefits as well as the dangers of not reading and studying the Word of GOD. Friends, of all of the book that are written and published in this world, the Bible, or the Word of GOD, is worth more than all of them put together.

Reading and studying all of the books of the world will not benefit you one bit when our Lord and Savior returns to claim those who have been given Him by GOD.

Remember the rich man, GOD, in His Word, referred to him as a fool for placing all of his heart into his riches. There are also people who have their hearts set on acquiring all of the knowledge of this world. I'm all for getting a good education, but with all your getting of this worlds knowledge, get more of the knowledge of GOD, read and study His Word, please.

Before I start to tell you of the Tricks of Satan, one for everyday of the week, I want to show you this scripture again that was used in a previous chapter but recorded by a different disciple. **Luke 9:25** says;

25) For what is a man profited, if he gain the whole world, and loose or forfeit his own soul.

I hope you don't take what I'm saying lightly. GOD does not take His Words lightly. He will hold us accountable for each Word. How do I know this? GOD says so in His Word. You'll do well if you start reading and studying His Word and find this out for your self.

Now let's see what tricks our enemy has up his sleeve. I hope and pray that as you read this chapter that your eyes are opened and your mind is clear. Everything that I'm about to tell you has been shown to me by GOD through the Holy Spirit as ways the enemy uses to cause people to commit sin without ever noticing it.

Are you ready? Here we go!

Trick #1—Television programs and Movies.

As I flipped through the seemingly long list of channels and programs, I came across a disturbing amount of sex and violence. I continued to flick the remote control and I saw a few programs that I once enjoyed. Now in a new light, a marvelous light, these same programs had become offensive to me.

You see by reading and studying the Word of GOD, the Holy Spirit, began a work in me, a work that teaches and brings an awareness of all things. The Word of GOD can do many things for a person who reads and receives it.

Because of the Word of GOD, I was able to see certain television programs and movies as they really are; tricks of the devil. Hold it right there, I said certain programs and movies. I'm talking about the programs or movies that depict illicit or explicit sex scenes.

These programs or movies play on the lust of our sinful nature to first catch our attention and then hold us in a state of sinful stupor. We, sometimes, while changing channels, are snagged by a program that we really had no intentions of watching, just because our eyes caught a glimpse of a sex scene.

Before you start to think that I am talking about programs that are referred to as pornography, let me give you an example. I am referring to programs that exploit men and women bodies. In most cases their not totally nude, but their apparel is of such that it will peak your interest. These are not unattractive men or woman. In fact the men are handsome and of course, the women are beautiful.

Now I want you to think about this before I go any further. Christians are still human beings. I don't want you to ever forget this because if you do, you may find yourself sitting between the twins, Sin and Shame.

Guys don't be naïve to the facts of life. Men are naturally attracted to woman. If you sit and allow yourself to be entertained by a beautiful nude or semi-nude woman, you will most likely desire her in your heart. Unless your, well I won't go there in this book.

You see this is a "Trick of the Trade" because Satan knows the Word of GOD. He was expelled from heaven, but, he still knows the Word of GOD. Just to prove to you that Satan knows the Word of GOD, here is a scripture in which a conversation between Jesus and Satan is recorded. **Matthew 4:6** reads;

> **6) And (Satan) saith unto him, If thou be the Son of God, cast thy self down, for it is written . . .**

I'll stop there because I want you to see that Satan is actually trying to tell Jesus what is written. The fact that Satan knows the Word of GOD or what is written, means that he can and will use the Word of GOD against us! I'll explain this more in-depth later.

As we sit and watch these seemingly harmless programs, we are in fact, sowing into our sinful nature without ever realizing it. I say that we are being tricked by this form of entertainment.

You see the Word of GOD explains all things to the reader by way of the Holy Spirit. I told you in the beginning of this chapter about what GOD said in **2ⁿᵈ Timothy 3:16**, that the Word of GOD was profitable in doctrine, for reproof, for correction . . . If you are doing something wrong, the Word of GOD will surely correct you.

When we blindly sit and watch the kinds of programs I described earlier, because we are all human with natural desires and attractions, we fall victim to Satan's tricks of the trade.

Brothers I'll use us as an example. The Word of God in **Matthew 5:28** say;

28) But I say unto you, that whosoever looketh on a woman to lust after her hath committed adultery with her already in his heart.

With this scripture in mind, examine why you watch certain programs or movies. Screen your television programs and movies as you would your telephone calls.

If you can indulge into these kinds of programs without being taken in by the beauty of the female actresses, or for you Sisters, be taken in by the handsome hunks, as you say. Then by all means, help yourself.

At least now that you've been told about this trick, you cannot be tricked into sinning, instead, you will have to make a conscious choice to, as the Word of GOD says; "sow into your corrupt nature".

Word of caution, **Galatians 6:7** says;

7) Be not deceived; God is not mocked: for whatsoever a man soweth, that shall he also reap.

Woman too!

Trick # 2—Music.

Satan seems to really be gaining momentum in this area. The music of today has really gotten out of hand. Some of the songs that are played on the radio stations also have an explicit version that is sold in the music stores.

I have, in the past, heard some songs with some really vulgar lyrics. The language used in today's music is laced with profanities and sexual innuendos.

Satan uses music, especially intended for our youths as a means of bringing his evil messages into the world, supposedly un-noticed. As I see the younger generation bounce to the beat of today's music, I perceive that they have no idea what's really going on. There is so much violence being portrayed in today's music that there are even songs with prerecorded gun shots mixed in.

Our youth, the future fathers and mothers of the next generations are being fed nothing short of pure evil. We must be careful not to allow ourselves and more importantly our youth to fall for this trick of Satan.

Of course there are scriptures that warn us about the evils of this world. We must read and study the Word of GOD to understand what is truly profitable and what's not.

I can testify as to how easy it is to listen to a recording or CD and actually believe that the lyrics are good sound advice. That the lyrics state what actually happens in life.

I have learned to be very careful as to what I allow to enter my eyes and ears. You must also be careful as to what you allow, and yes, you have the choice as to what is received into your ears.

Please be careful as to what you allow to be received into your ears, processed by your mind and entered into your heart.

The Word of GOD gives us a lot of information for our benefit, or as the scripture says; to be profitable. There is a scripture that states we must be careful whose table we sit and eat at. We are being told not to just sit looking or listening to whatever is placed before us. Indeed this is a warning that we can't afford to just sit and listen to anything and everything that's out there in the world.

Friends, Brothers, Sisters, for GOD sake, don't forget who's out there; going to and fro, seeking whom he may devour. The ruler of this world is out there. His job description will never change. Even his music has all of the elements of his evil intentions, to steal, kill and destroy.

It's sad that we have the solutions to all of life's troubles but don't use them. What am I saying? Please read and study the Word of GOD for yourself.

Trick #3—False gods or Religions.

Do I have to? O.K. Since you don't want to be tricked by Satan into going to Hell, because you wasted your life serving a false god or being part of a false religion, I'll spend a little more time on this subject.

If your memory serves you correctly, this was the subject matter in the first chapter of this book. This subject is evidence that these two tricks really do exist.

The name of this trick tells you that it is a reality.

In other words, there are people who worship false gods and practice false religions. If you are not careful they will encourage you to fall victim to the same deceptions or trickery they've fallen into.

As I read and studied the Word of GOD, in the Old Testament. I saw how the people of old would turn away from the God of Abraham, Isaac and Jacob and the consequences they suffered for doing so. At times as I read, I would become angry at these people in light of the blessings that they received from GOD and also the miracles that were performed right before their very eyes. These people blindly turned away from GOD and worshiped gods that were false.

In the Word of GOD we can find yet another clear warning. **Deuteronomy 11:16** says;

16) Take heed to yourselves, that your heart be not deceived, and ye turn aside, and serve other gods, and worship them.

I don't think I need to try to explain this scripture, do you? It would appear as if GOD is telling it like it is. We can see that GOD knows that there are false gods in the world. Why else would He warn us? I hope by now you are really beginning to understand how important it is to read and study the Word of GOD.

Also I want to show you a scripture about false religions and what our Lord and Savior, Jesus Christ, had to say about them. **Matthew 4:10**;

> **10) Then saith Jesus unto him, Get thee hence, Satan: for it is written, THOU SHALT WORSHIP THE LORD THY GOD, AND HIM ONLY SHALT THOU SERVE.**

Here's a question. In your religion, do you worship the Lord thy GOD? If you answer no to this question, then I can truthfully tell you that are part of a false religion. Enough said.

Trick #4—Drugs and Alcohol Abuse.

I refer to these two subjects as tricks of the trade because of the word abuse. The abuse of drugs and alcohol has made a large contribution to the destruction of mankind.

Drugs such as Marijuana, Cocaine and Heroin are nicknamed as street drugs. These drugs are just a few of the arsenal of weapons the enemy has at his disposal. These drugs are often used for the first time by means of pier pressure. You know, Come on man; just try it once!

The transfer from use to abuse varies with each individual, but the outcome or end result is always the same, NOT GOOD. If used and then abused at a young enough age they can hinder a person from naturally developing a healthy and positive self-esteem. Through the abuse of drugs and alcohol, Satan, has most definitely followed the directives listed in his job description, to steal, kill and destroy.

He has introduced drugs and alcohol into our society with the foreknowledge that mankind, some, will use these things at first, experimentally and later detrimentally. For sure, drugs and alcohol abuse are to be seen and understood as tricks of the trade.

People go from trying these things once, in some cases, to dependence upon them. Remember the slogan, "Try it you'll like it". This catchy slogan, like a lot of things, can be used by Satan to trick a person into falling for one his tricks. Satan and his trick of drugs and alcohol abuse has stolen people's hard earned money, killed their bodies and eventually destroyed their souls. Not to mention, marriages have been destroyed, jobs lost and crimes committed.

How can we as well as our children avoid these tricks? We must turn to our Lord and Savior Jesus

Christ and humbly ask him to remove, if we have already been tricked into trying these things or keep us, through His Word, from being tempted to try these things.

In the Word of GOD, we can, as I mentioned before, find the right solutions to all of life's troubles. While I was reading and studying the Word of GOD, I found out how Jesus Christ handled being tempted or tricked by the devil. In the book of **Matthew**, starting at **the 4th chapter and 1st verse**, the Word of GOD says;

1) Then was Jesus led up of the spirit into the wilderness to be tempted of the devil.

This scripture is very important to us as clearly describes the devil as being the one who tempts us. Reading and studying the Word of GOD can combat the onslaught of Satan's lies as well as temptations. The next scripture will show you what our Lord and Savior did to silence to mouth of Satan. Once again from the book of **Matthew 4:4**;

4) But he answered, It is written, Man shall not live by bread alone, but by every word that proceedth out of out of the mouth of God.

I ask you, what is every word that proceedth out of the mouth of GOD, except, the Word of GOD. We must read and study His Word in order for us to be able to use it against Satan when he tries to tempt us. Not only do we need to read and study the Word of GOD, we also need to encourage our children to do likewise. Just saying no is not enough!

Trick #5—Your five senses.

As mentioned earlier in this book, I told you that your or should I say our, five senses were given to us while we live in these fleshly bodies. This is so that we can deal with the natural world around us. I reminded you of this fact to explain to you that Satan can also use our five senses to trick us.

Through the use of our five senses he can and will trick us out of our blessings, healings or receiving answers to our prayers. Indeed our five senses can also be used to trick us into believing the lies of Satan instead of the truths of GOD.

In the New Testament, there is a scripture that very well illustrates how our five senses, if placed in a higher priority, than the truths stated in the Word of GOD, can work against us.

Still, in the book of Matthew, we can read all about how Jesus fed more than five thousand people with five loaves of bread and two fish. What I want to show you is what happened afterwards. In **Matthew 14:22 to 31**, the Word of GOD says;

> **22) And straightway Jesus constrained his disciples to get into a ship, and to go before him unto the other side, while he sent the multitudes away.**

> **23) And when he had sent the multitudes away, he went up into a mountain apart to pray: and when the evening was come, he was there alone.**

> **24) But the ship was now in the midst of the sea, tossed with waves: for the wind was contrary.**

> **25) And in the fourth watch of the night Jesus went unto them, walking on the sea.**

> **26) And when the disciples saw him walking on the sea, they were troubled, saying, It is a spirit; and they cried out for fear.**

> **27) But straightway Jesus spake unto them, saying, Be of good cheer; it is I; be not afraid.**

28) And Peter answered him and said, Lord, if it be thou, bid me come unto thee on the water.

29) And he said, Come. And when Peter was come down out of the ship, he walked on the water, to go to Jesus.

30) But when he saw the wind boisterous, he was afraid: and beginning to sink, he cried, saying, Lord, save me.

31) And immediately Jesus stretched forth his hand, and caught him, and said unto him, O thou of little faith, wherefore didst thou doubt?

Friends, these scriptures provide us with proof that at least one of our five senses can be used against us. In the scriptures you have just read, Peter, upon seeing our Lord and Savior walking on the water, challenged Him by saying, **Lord if it be thou, bid me come unto thee on the water**, and that's exactly what Jesus did. Peter, being focused on Jesus, what He said, **Come,** stepped down from the ship onto, not into, the water and began to walk on top of the water to meet Him.

Then something happened (although this is not written, Satan created a diversion, or trick) which caused Peter to take his eyes and mind off of the faith, trust and belief, that he had in Jesus' Word, or for the sake of your understanding, the Word of GOD.

You see Peter allowed himself to place more trust in at least one of his five senses than he did in Jesus. This can be confirmed by Jesus' response to Peter sinking into the sea. After Jesus caught Peter's hand, saving him, Jesus in the form of a question, told Peter and us exactly why he started to sink. Jesus simply said, **O thou of little faith, wherefore didst thou doubt?**

What I want you to understand is that you cannot allow your five senses to govern your spiritual relationship with GOD. I pray that you learn to use your spiritual eyes and ears to define your relationship with GOD.

When you start to read and study the Word of God you will be made aware of all of the tricks of Satan. I've found that it doesn't help a whole lot for me in my walk with GOD, to pay a lot of attention to my physical being, situation or circumstance.

In fact, the Word of GOD tells us exactly how we are to walk in this world. Using one of our five senses as an example, we are told in **2nd Corinthians, 5th chapter and 7th verse;**

7) For we walk by faith, and not by sight.

We need to read and study the Word of GOD and allow GOD, through His Word, to lead us and guide us through life here on earth. Through the Word of GOD and our faith, trust and belief in it, we will not fall for the tricks that our enemy uses against us.

If we ask GOD for something, whatsoever, that is within His will, we will loose out if we base our receiving whatsoever on what we see, hear, smell, taste or feel. We must ignore our five senses, as in the case of asking for healing, not allow how we feel to over-ride our faith and trust in GOD, or His Word.

Reading and studying the Word of GOD will tell you how to receive your blessings, healings and salvation, also, how to see the tricks of Satan.

Trick #6—Fear, Doubt and Worry.

Don't look so surprised! These tricks of the trade are common in believers as well as in people who could care less about the Word of GOD. Through the use of fear, doubt or worry, Satan can trick a person into not doing what they should do, or doing what they should not do.

The Word of GOD gives a person confidence. I can honestly testify of this in my own life. Being able to write this book is a fruit of that confidence.

Don't think that Satan hasn't tried to use of these and many other tricks against me. This book was actually given to me to write in 1998 and I wrote it. To bring it to reality I have in a lot of ways gone through pure Hell. Only through prayer, along with reading and studying the Word of GOD was I able to recognize, understand and overcome these tricks.

The confidence given to me through the Word of GOD has cancelled out the affects of fear, doubt and worry. In the Word of GOD, we are told point blank, that we were not given a spirit of fear.

In **2nd Timothy, chapter 1, verse 7**, the Word of GOD says;

7) For God has not given us the spirit of fear; but of power, and of love, and of a sound mind.

As you can see in His Word, GOD tells us the truth. The Word of GOD covers every subject under the Sun, past, present and future.

The trick of fear is what keeps people from, as the U.S. Army's advertisings say; Be all you can be.

Satan is quick to use this trick against us to keep us from reaching our true and full potentials. He also uses doubt and worry very much in the same way as he uses fear, to hinder us.

When you don't read and study the Word of GOD and learn the truth, Satan, through his tricks of the trade, will walk all over you as you strive to prosper.

GOD, in His Word, has shown me these tricks and also shown me whom I should fear. From **Matthew 10:28**, GOD warns;

28) And fear not them which kill the body, but are not able to kill the soul: but rather fear him which is able to destroy both soul and body in hell.

Never forget that Satan is a liar. Don't allow him to use his knowledge of the Word of GOD against you. Read and study the Word of GOD for yourself.

I ask you to do this so that you can receive all that GOD has promised you in His Word. Our enemy knows that doubt will render your prayers null and void. One more thing, Worry; I'll sum this up in a saying that tells you how we should view worry.

"If you are going to worry, don't pray. If you are going to pray, then don't worry. Understand?

Trick #7—The Word of GOD.

Even now while I write these words I can hear some of you screaming; Oh No! Brother Swinton, you've gone too far! All through this book you have been stressing to us how important it is for us to read and study the Word of GOD, and now you tell us it is a trick of the devil?

In my defense, I will clarify what I mean by this eyebrow raising statement. All I'm saying is that, Satan will, because of your lack of knowledge of the Word of GOD, use it against you. I hope you haven't already rent your clothes. GOD knew that this trick would come as a surprise to some of you and that's why He has saved it for last.

There is no reason for you to be surprised by this trick unless you can admit that you have not been reading and studying the Word of GOD. I want to show you some scriptures that will explain to you how Satan will try to use the Word of God to deceive you. Before doing so, I want to ask you to read these scriptures very slowly and rightly divide the Word of GOD, so that your understanding is clear.

While writing this book I used the **King James Version** to give you scriptures. There are many translations of the Word of GOD that have been written in a more modern form of the English language. For the most part, I believe that these more modern translations follow the King James Version very closely.

What I am saying is I feel that it is O.K. to read and study the Word of GOD using a more modern translation if it is easier for you to understand. I mentioned earlier that if you ever have a hard time understanding what is written, you should stop right where you are and ask GOD, in the name of Jesus Christ, to give you or bless you, with a clear understanding of His Word.

Having said that, I'll begin with the Word of GOD from **John 1:1st thru the 14th verses**;

1) **In the beginning was the Word, and the Word was with God, and the Word was God.**

2) **The same was in the beginning with God.**

3) **All things were made by him: and without him was not any thing made that was made.**

4) In him was life: and the life was the light of men.

5) And the light shineth in darkness; and the darkness comprehended it not.

6) There was a man sent from God, whose name was John.

7) The same came for a witness, to bear witness of the Light, that all men through him might believe.

8) He was not that Light, but was sent to bear witness of that Light.

9) That was the true Light, which lighteth every man that cometh into the world.

10) He was in the world, and the world was made by him, and the world knew him not.

11) He came unto his own, and his own received him not.

12) But as many as received him, to them gave he power to become the sons of God, even to them that believe on his name:

13) Which were born, not of blood, nor of the will of the flesh, nor of the will of man, but of God.

14) And the Word was made flesh, and dwelt among us, (and we beheld his glory as of the only begotten of the Father,) full of grace and truth.

As I was typing these scriptures, I thought to myself, this is one way to get people to read and study the Word of GOD. In **John 1:1 thru 14**, we are given a lot of information we really need to know and believe. In particular is the scripture about the Word of GOD being made flesh, **verse 14**.

This scripture is referring to none other than our Lord and Savior, Jesus Christ. There is much more information given than this but I only want to focus on this particular fact. Jesus Christ was the Word, of GOD, made flesh.

Keeping in mind what the Word has to say concerning Jesus I want you to see why it is so important for you to read and study the Word of GOD.

Do you know that even though, Jesus Christ was the Word made flesh, our enemy, Satan, still tried to trick Him? In **Matthew 4:5 to 7,** the Word of GOD says;

5) Then the devil taketh him up into the holy city, and setteth him on a pinnacle of the temple,

6) And saith unto him, If thou be the Son of God, cast thy self down, for it is written, He shall give his angels charge concerning thee: and in their hands they shall bear thee up, lest at any time thou dash thy foot against a stone.

7) Jesus said unto him, It is written again, Thou shalt not tempt the Lord thy God.

Friends, the first time I read this I was truly amazed. I thought to myself, of all the nerve, Satan, the liar, was trying to tell Jesus Christ, what is written.

And get this, Satan, was actually quoting what is written in the Word of GOD. The actual scripture he tried to trick Jesus with can be found in **Psalms 91:11 and 12**.

11) For he shall give his angels charge over thee to keep thee in all thy ways.

12) They shall bear thee up in their hands, lest thou dash thy foot against a stone.

Here is a thought. If Satan is so low down and dirty as well as being bold enough to try to use the Word of God against our Lord and Savior, then he won't hesitate for a hot second to use it against us. As if you stood much of a chance since you don't read and study the Word of GOD, daily. I'm sorry, I couldn't help myself and it was just too easy.

Why do you think GOD, through the Holy Spirit, has given me this book to write? It's because He wants people to read and study His Word so that you will, among other things, know all of the tricks of the trade that the enemy desires to use against you.

In His Word, GOD is careful to tell us all that we need to know to prosper in this life.

Today is Easter Sunday and as I went into the House of Prayer, the Church, I saw many people carrying Bibles in their hands. I had to wonder to myself how many of these people had just picked up their Bibles this morning, for the first time this week. I ask that you please set aside a few minutes each day, morning, noon or night to read and study the Word of GOD for yourself. I can guarantee that GOD, can and will, keep you and bless you, through His Word.

I have a sister named Winifred who has been and still is blessed by reading and studying the Word of GOD. Some years ago she gave me a Bible as a gift. It was a beautiful black leather Bible trimmed in gold with my name inscribed on the front in gold. To my shame, I must admit that I allowed the enemy to steal that Bible from me. I have no idea whatsoever where it is now. I used to worry about it a lot but I've gotten past that now. I can only hope and pray that whoever has it, is putting it to good use, by reading and studying the Word of GOD.

As I come to the end of this chapter, I sincerely hope that the messages contained in this chapter have fallen on good ground deep within you. Have taken root and will grow up within you, mind, body and soul and also produce good fruit to the glory of the Kingdom of GOD.

Well Brothers and Sisters, there you have it, one trick for every day of the week. As I said before I hope you weren't too surprised to hear about these tricks, but if you were, that's good; No that's great! It means that now you have been made aware of how crafty and cunning our enemy really is.

Making you aware of these tricks has made this chapter a lot of joy for me. I've really enjoyed it because I believe in GOD and in the power of His Word.

I want you to look at this book as being a sort of flashlight, to help you see better in the darkness that is in this world. By the way, you will never have to change the batteries because this book is powered by the Word of God.

One last thing, I want even Satan himself to hear this. The Word of GOD says in the book of **Proverbs 1:17**;

17) Surely in vain the net is spread in the sight of any bird.

Friends, you have no excuses, you have been shown the net. Simply fly around it!

Chapter #9

Don't Be No Fool

Believe it or not, the title of this chapter has both, nothing to do with the title of this book and at the same time, it has everything to do with the title of this book. Confused? Hopefully you won't be when you get to the end of this chapter.

Heavenly Father, I thank you for inspiring me to not only write this book, but boldly express to the reader, these messages that you have revealed to me by your Holy Spirit. I thank you and praise you in the name of Jesus Christ. Amen.

Have you ever heard the expression; a fool and his money soon part? It's true! I know because I've been there and to complete the saying, done that. To tell you the truth, I felt like a fool.

What I want to tell you about is what the Word of GOD has to say about the word fool. There are many scriptures given concerning this simple four letter word. There is even a warning from GOD in his Word in regard to the use of the word fool. **Matthew 5:22** says;

22) But I say unto you, That whosoever is angry with his brother without a cause shall be in danger of the judgment: and whosoever shall say to his brother, Ra'-ca, shall be in danger of the council: but whosoever shall say, Thou fool, shall be in danger of hell fire.

In this scripture, specifically, in the last part, we are clearly being told not say to anyone; you fool. So please let's not do this.

While I was writing this book I felt, and still do, privileged to have been led by GOD through the Holy Spirit to do this. To me this is the best thing that I have been able to do so far, in my life. Almighty GOD has used this book to not only show me, but also tell me how blessed I really am.

As I wrote the rough draft of this book I had a roommate. During one of our conversations he confessed to me that he was not totally convinced that GOD really did exist. I really shouldn't tell you how this made me feel. The truth is, some days I almost did not like him. Each day however, GOD blessed me with enough love for him to last until the next day and so on.

My roommate later said to me that maybe he thought and felt the way he did because of his up-bringing. As I listened to him, I understood that his parents did not attend church. Just by hearing him say these things to me my heart went out to him. From then on, every chance I got I tried to throw in a plug for GOD.

At one point even what our Lord and Savior Jesus Christ said entered my mind. **Matthew 10:14**;

14) And whosoever shall not receive you, nor hear your words, when ye depart out of that house or city, shake off the dust of your feet.

I believe that this was to be a testimony against them or whoever would not heed the Word of GOD that is spoken to them.

Anyway, I developed a love for my roommate that could have only come from GOD, a love for the salvation of his eternal soul. I prayed for my roommate that he would come into the knowledge of the truth and be saved. In spite of his confessions, I still had hope.

I guess I find it hard to believe that there are people, especially in the southeastern part of

America, or even those of us who live in the Bible Belt, that don't believe in GOD.

I thought to myself, how in the world could such a thing happen? I settled down and began to compare our backgrounds.

We are men of about the same age. We were both born and raised in the Southeast. We have also shared similar experiences in life. So what was or could have been the deciding factor. You tell me.

I was born in Charleston, South Carolina. As a kindergarten student I was taught the **23rd Psalm**. I lost both my parents at the age of six years old and was then raised by my loving GOD fearing grandmother.

My dear sweet grandmother lived to be 108 years old. In fact, my grandmother was also the mother of our church. She raised my older half-brother, my sister and I. What kept her going all of those years? I believe it was her faith, trust and belief in GOD Almighty. She also allowed herself to be used by GOD to be a blessing to others, not to mention, she had applied the Word of GOD in her life, even in how she raised us.

In the book of Proverbs, we can find a scripture that offers Godly wisdom to parents, or in my case, grandparents. **Proverbs 22:6** says;

6) Train up a child in the way he should go: and when he is old, he will not depart from it.

To testify on my grandmothers' behalf I can proudly and honestly state the following in truth. She would get my sister and me up for Sunday school. We didn't just go to Sunday school; we also went to church, sometimes all day, even at night. She took us to revivals, programs, gospel singings, camp meetings and big meetings.

As you can see, she did exactly what the Word of GOD said that parents should do and she has been greatly rewarded with long life. I thank and praise my lord and Savior Jesus Christ for allowing me to have had a grandmother that believed in GOD Almighty and His Word.

Now is as good a time as any to ask you to please read and study the Word of GOD for yourself, and apply it in your life. This will be a blessing to you as well as your children or as in my case, your children's children.

Remember my roommate? Well his parents didn't do what my dear grandmother did. I prayed for my roommate. I hope he comes into the knowledge of GOD Almighty and receives a double portion of the Holy Ghost. Hey! God can do whatever He wants to do. I don't know what the future holds but GOD knows.

In the Word of GOD we can find a scripture that speaks about people who don't believe in GOD. **Psalm 53:1**, the Word of GOD says;

1) **The fool has said in his heart, there is no God. Corrupt are they, and have done abominable iniquity: there is none that doeth good.**

We can surely see by this scripture that a person, who does not believe in GOD, or an Atheist, is to be considered as a fool.

Now as far as my roommate is concerned, and this is the honest truth, GOD allowed me to see him, on more than one occasion, read and study the Word of GOD. The first time I saw him do this, I tried to keep my cool but I couldn't. I looked at him with a hearty grin and said, "Praise the Lord! In response, he looked up at me with an innocently humble smile and went right back to reading.

I don't know how he felt, but I truly felt good for him.

All in all, our Lord and Savior Jesus Christ, gets all the glory, honor and praise for what I saw as a miracle. For someone, whom confessed to not believing in GOD, who read novels and magazines all the time, to out of the clear blue sky, begin to read and study the Word of GOD, I call that a miracle.

Thank you Jesus, if in someway, I did or said something that inspired my roommate to read and study the Word of GOD. For you, the reader, I also hope that this book inspires you to read and study the Word of GOD for yourself.

I will be praying to GOD, in the name of Jesus, that you do. I can assure you of this one thing, I won't worry about it after I pray about it. Remember, if your going to worry, don't pray; if your going to pray, don't worry.

Friends, before ending this chapter, I must ask you again to please read and study the Word of GOD for yourself. Don't you fall into doubt about the existence of GOD Almighty, GOD is real, His name is Jesus Christ and so is the Holy Spirit.

You must read and study the Word of GOD to find the truth about any and all of your questions, concerns or doubts. GOD is the creator of heaven and earth and the fullness thereof. He wants us to not only believe in Him but have faith and trust in Him as well. He stands ready, willing and able to love us, help us and save us.

Here is a scripture found in the book of Hosea. **Hosea 14:9** says;

9) Who is wise, and he shall understand these things? prudent, and he shall know them? for the ways of the Lord are right, and the just shall walk in them: but the transgressors shall fall therein.

By this scripture we find that a person is considered wise if he or she applies their understanding to the ways of the Lord, prudent, if they know them. When a person reads and studies the Word of GOD, they are blessed with an understanding and knowledge of GOD. This will render that person both prudent and wise.

We've already read and studied what GOD has to say about people who don't believe in Him. These people are referred to as being fools, remember?

That's why I believe that GOD has blessed me with both the title of this book; Don't Be no Fool, please Read and Study the Word of GOD: and the title of this particular chapter.

As the title of this book has a message, so does the title of this chapter. Don't allow yourself to be classified or counted with the unbelievers of this world. In other words; **Don't Be No Fool.**

Chapter #10

Now You Know

Well friends, I'm sorry to report to you that this is the final chapter of this book. I must admit that I have really enjoyed being able to share my beliefs and understanding of the Word of GOD with you, while encouraging you to read and study the Word of GOD, for yourself.

I shall begin this final chapter with a prayer of thanksgiving.

Heavenly and merciful Father, first of all please allow me to thank you. Thank you for allowing me to humble myself in your presence and bow down before your Throne of Grace. Thank you for blessing me with praise on my lips and a song of praise in my heart. Thank you for removing my feet from destruction and snatching me back from the gates of Death and Hell.

Thank you Father for blessing me with a Spirit of Willing Obedience and the gift of the Holy Spirit, the speaking in an unknown tongue as the Spirit gives me the utterance. Thank you for blessing me with perfect health and excellent strength. Thank you for leading and guiding me in the right direction. Thank you for creating in me a clean heart and making me a new creature.

Thank you, Heavenly Father for your Plan of Salvation. Thank you for your love that allowed you to send you're only begotten Son into the world, to suffer and die for my sins and the sins of the entire world. Thank you for the precious blood of Jesus Christ that was shed on the Cross of Calvary that cleanses me from all unrighteousness. Thank you for the stripes he bore which healed me from all manner of sickness and disease.

Thank you Heavenly Father for your Word that I can stand on and is a solid foundation. Thank you for teaching me how to pray.

Thank you for blessing me with wisdom, knowledge and understanding of your Word and your way. Thank you Heavenly Father just for being you, and allowing me to return to you as the Prodigal Son. Thank you for greeting me and embracing me with your loving arms around me.

Heavenly Father, I also thank you for all the many wonderful blessings that you have bestowed upon me and for blessing me to see with spiritual eyes and hear with spiritual ears. Thank you for prompting me to write this book and allowing me to be a blessing to all those that I may encounter, be it in word or deed. Thank you for those that you have placed in my life to help me.

Oh! Heavenly Father, now I wish to praise you for hearing this prayer of Thanksgiving.

Heavenly Father I praise you, I glorify you, I magnify you. You are the only GOD; there is no other before you. You are the creator of heaven and earth and the fullness thereof.

Holy, Holy, Holy is the Lord GOD Almighty. I worship you, I say HALLELUJAH, even glory HALLELUJAH to your praise. You are the one and only, true and wise GOD, who is able to do things that are far exceedingly and abundantly above, all that we may ask or think.

Bless the Lord. O, my soul and all that is within me. Bless His Holy name. Thank you Father GOD, thank you, thank you. Praise you Father GOD.

Heavenly Father, I thank you and praise you, in the name of my Lord and Savior, Jesus Christ. Amen.

Friends, it has been a privilege to share with you all of the scriptures that GOD has given me to use in the writing of this book. I believe that GOD Almighty has blessed me with the ability to write this book.

The title of this book; **Don't Be No Fool, Read and Study the Word of GOD for Yourself**, is the reoccurring message that can be found in each chapter. Truly this is not only the message but good sound advice.

The Words of GOD are all true, every story, every miracle, every promise as well as every warning. GOD has given us His Word for us to apply it in our lives. GOD's Word is based on His wisdom, knowledge and understandings. Indeed no one is wiser.

When you or anyone reads and studies the Word of GOD, GOD exposes the reader to privileged information that is not top secret or even classified. GOD, not being a respecter of person has openly exposed us to His sacred teachings. Why? It is my belief that He loves us dearly and wants us to get to know Him.

GOD, in His Word, tells us of how He has helped those in need, instructed the simple, defended the weak, brought the dead back to life, restored sight to the blind, healed the sick, sacrificed His only Son and given salvation to all that believe in Him.

Of course, we must read and study His Word to find out all that our Heavenly Father wants us to know and believe.

The Word of GOD is as described in the scripture **John 17:17**;

17) Sanctify them through thy truth; thy word is truth.

This scripture is yet another confirmation that the Words of GOD are all true, whether we choose to believe Him or not. When you do read and study the Word of GOD and find out the consequences of not believing, you may reevaluate your thinking. I say this in support of the following scripture, **Hebrews 4:12** says;

12) For the Word of God is quick, and powerful, and sharper than any twoedged sword, piercing even to the dividing asunder of soul and spirit, and of the joints and marrow, and is a discerner of the thoughts and intents of the heart.

Any questions? This scripture separates the Word of GOD from any and all literary works available to mankind. Indeed the Word of GOD is just that, the Words that GOD has spoken to those chosen to receive and record His Words.

In the book of Ephesians we are being told that we should take the Word of GOD with us to protect us and combat the lies of Satan. **Ephesians 6:17** says;

17) And take the helmet of salvation, and the sword of the Spirit, which is the word of God:

In this scripture when it says that we should take the Word of GOD with us, it is understood that we are to take it with us in our hearts and not only in our hands. This means that we must read and study the Word of GOD until it becomes a part of us, mind, body and soul.

In the beginning of **Chapter #8, Tricks of the Trade**, I told you that GOD does not take His Words lightly, that He will hold us accountable for each word.

Here is the scripture that tells us without any doubts how GOD will use His Word against those who don't read and study His Word and apply it their lives. **Revelation 2:16** says;

16) Repent; or else I will come unto thee quickly, and will fight against them with the sword of my mouth.

In this scripture the Word of GOD is being referred to as; the sword of my mouth.

Friends, once again, please read and study the Word of GOD so that you can benefit from it. GOD so desperately wants us to prosper in this life as well as spend eternity in His glory.

It's not right that our Lord and Savior Jesus Christ, was crucified, buried and arose on the third day, now seated at the right hand of GOD Almighty, making intersession for us and you not know it, believe it or receive it.

I would, if given a choice between knowing my own name and reading and studying the Word of GOD to believe and receive all that GOD has in store for me, would, without hesitation, forget who in the world, Brother William Swinton is. Why you may ask?

The Word of GOD in the book of **Jeremiah, chapter 15 and the 16th verse** says it all;

16) Thy Words were found, and I did eat them; and thy Word was unto me the joy

and rejoicing of mine heart: for I am called by thy name, O Lord God of hosts.

Glory HALLELUJAH!!!

Brothers and Sisters I could go on and on about how important it is for us to read and study the Word of GOD. Taking into consideration that you will heed the message of this book, I know you can't wait to get started.

I have told everything that I believe GOD has given me to say through the Holy Spirit.

You no longer have any excuses for not reading and studying the Word of GOD. In other words, as in the title of this chapter; Now You Know.

One more thing before I end this chapter. I'm sure you've heard the sayings, these are the last and evil days; these are the times that try men souls and that we need to stand the test of time.

Keeping these sayings in mind, I offer this question.

To know that there will be a test and not study for it is something a fool would do, right?

Then I say to you with a sincere love and hope that you take to heart the title of this book; **Don't Be No Fool, please Read and Study the Word of GOD for yourself.**

Letter to the Reader

My Dearest Reader,

Praise the Lord!! I hope and pray that this book has been a blessing to you as it has been and is to me.

To tell you the truth, this book came to me at a time in my life when I was going through one of the most difficult situations I had ever faced.

Literally being knocked down to the ground, I could only draw on what I had been raised to know and believe. That there is a GOD and I was not alone in my troubles. That GOD, whose name is Jesus Christ, was there for me and also with me and had the power to bring me through, as well as out of the darkest of situations.

Not really knowing what I was doing, it came to me to start reading the Bible. I was to the point that I didn't even know where or what to read so I decided to read the entire Bible. This was something that I had always wanted to do anyway and now was the perfect time. I had nothing to loose.

Before I began to read the Bible I asked GOD to lead and guide me through my Bible studies. A thought came to me to write down all of the names of the books of the Old Testament on a single sheet of paper.

Afterwards, I cut out each book name into a single strip of paper, much like preparation for pulling names at Christmas time. I placed all of the folded little pieces of paper into a container, shook them up, prayed over it and accepted that what ever piece of paper or book of the Bible came out of the container was what I was supposed to read and so on.

I repeated this same process as I finished all of the books of the Old Testament and began to read the New Testament.

Naturally, I was not reading and studying the Bible in its present order, from Genesis to Revelation. My Bible study was completely out of order. Nevertheless, I completely read and studied the entire Bible.

As I was in the process of reading the Bible, a feeling, or if you will, a Spirit, came over me that I cannot fully describe to you or to myself. This was in 1999 and I still remember it like it was yesterday. At times I felt like I couldn't even take a deep breath.

Once my readings were completed, I started to write. Now, I don't mean to say that this was something I purposed to do, I was compelled to write. First the title of this book came to me, then the titles of all ten chapters. All of this took place in about five minutes.

For some reason I knew what every title of each chapter would speak about and the content of the chapter. After the outline, over the next few days and nights I could not stop writing. It was coming out of my mind so fast that I could hardly keep up. I wrote so much until a knot arose on my finger but I don't remember any pain associated with it. Oh! My GOD!!

As I mentioned before I was actually in the middle of a dark situation in my life during all of this. I had also completely forgotten about my situation, although I was still in it, it seemed not to be so dark after all.

Soon, after the situation or storm passed, the Sun came out again, brighter than ever.

Over the past several years I have had my personal trials, tests and tribulations just like everyone else and if it's one thing that I have learned it's this. No matter what or how bad things may be or even look; this too shall pass and there is a blessing in the storm.

This book is as the scripture says; **For GOD; is a rewarder of them that diligent seek Him**. In other words this book is just one of my rewards. Just as promised by GOD, I claim this reward in the name of my Lord and Savior, Jesus Christ.

Well, since God will always have the last Word, here it is. In the **Book of Acts; Chapter 2, verse 38**; we find the instructions to being saved.

Then Peter said unto them, Repent, and be baptized every one of you in the name of Jesus Christ for the remission of sins, and ye shall receive the gift of the Holy Ghost.

This is the exact way that God wants all of us to be baptized, In Jesus' name! Some churches will baptize you in the name of the Father, Son and Holy Ghost . . . These are Titles and not the name. Peter told the people exactly what God wanted them to do and they received exactly what the scriptures said they would. How do I know this? Because as a result of me being baptized in the name of Jesus Christ I also received the Gift of the Holy Ghost just as promised in the scriptures. I will never ever forget that day!

Please pay close attention to how the church you attend does things. Are they following God's Word, or are they following their own man-made traditions. I urge you to PLEASE take the words of this book to heart. Your eternal destiny is at stake. Amen.

Written in Love,
Brother William A. Swinton